## Pre-Publication Praise for *Women Fa...*

It was with great interest that I took up this ... might speak to my life and to the lives of the won... I am in my mid-fifties—nearer to retirement tha... ...o think and soon to be a part of the social phenomenon so aptly described in this book as "the empty desk syndrome."

Women have been working outside the home for decades, and millions have already retired. However, never before have so many been on the precipice of this transition with numerous reasonably healthy years left to live. Much has been written about the health-care needs of the expanding elder population—and about their economic status, housing choices, travel preferences, voting habits and what they will buy and from whom. Very little light has been shed on the topic of modern women in retirement. This book is a beacon that brings light to that subject and guidance to the women who are fortunate enough to read it as they move through this important and under-recognized life change.

On these pages you will encounter the stories of women who have breezed into retirement and found joyful freedom and relaxation, just as they thought the would. And you will read about many more who have found unexpected sadness or depression instead, and have no idea what to name it, let alone how to deal with it.

One of my roles as a psychiatrist is to facilitate healing from depression. Sometimes that can be accomplished by helping the person reframe the problem by viewing it within a larger social context. I will use this book as a tool to accomplish that task.

Whatever your gender, age, or walk of life, this book will take you on a journey filled with delightful stories and valuable insights. The exercises at the end are an added bonus and bestow practical value beyond the thought provoking message of the text itself.

—Gail Clinton, M.D.
Psychiatrist

This invaluable book deals with the manifold transitions of retirement. Its many case studies show retirement to be an adventure, and allow readers to learn from the experiences of their sisters. The exercises, in particular, give tools for emotional and psychological preparation. In short: I will buy this book for all my friends, whatever their ages.

—Chandra Watkins
Development Director
www.gratefulness.org

I just finished reading an advance copy of *Women Facing Retirement*, and really loved it! Even though I retired from paid employment years ago, when my congressman boss lost an election and I decided to start having kids, I can still relate to it. I too get caught up in busy routines, as people do in their jobs, and use work as an excuse not to think. And as my youngest leaves home, and my job description changes, I too feel a great loss. In my opinion, stories are the most interesting part of life, and the stories in this book are wonderful, well written, and interwoven with the author's wisdom. But the most powerful thing about this book is that it is written in the first person plural. Wow, what a wonderful feeling that gives me. I feel connected and understood. I feel a sense of sisterhood, and I feel hugged. This is a work of love destined to help a great many people.

—Anna Wolfe, Founder and President
The Mandala Center

I'm thankful that I read Bonnie Bostrom's encouraging, delicately instructive guide to retirement. Her commitment to helping women make retirement a great time in their lives resonates throughout every chapter. I took to heart each story, each voice, and felt comforted by the truthful and inspirational journey of every woman. I'm now beginning to picture myself in a different future, to see retirement as an opportunity to connect and reconnect with the parts of myself lost in the mundane business of living.

I will give this book to my mother, and to my girlfriends to give to their mothers. And I will begin my eventual retirement journey into healing and wholeness "with grace and agility," Bonnie Bostrom style.

—Elizabeth Shoemaker, M.S., Marriage and Family Therapist

I adored this book! I have been retired for over 20 years and still found it to be relevant to my life. It was a pleasure to read the stories and poetry of such diverse women. They write intimately and openly and are as inspiring to me now as they would have been when I was beginning my retirement. To this day I miss having meaningful work to do. Retirement is not something you get over. It is a life changing event that dictates the rest of your life and does not go away. *Women Facing Retirement* has given me a great sense of comfort because I know that others understand. I am going to do some of the exercises in the back, because this book has given me renewed optimism and enthusiasm about my own life.

—Heather Ragsdale, Retired Businesswoman

# Women Facing Retirement

## A Time for Self-Reflection

**Bonnie S. Bostrom**

with

Barbara Reider, Ph.D.

Aslan
PUBLISHING
Fairfield, CT

**Aslan Publishing**
2490 Black Rock Turnpike, #342
Fairfield, CT 06825
Please contact the publisher for a free catalog.
Phone: **203/372-0300**
Fax: **203/374-4766**
**www.aslanpublishing.com**

Library of Congress Cataloging-in-Publication Data

Bostrom, Bonnie S.
  Women facing retirement : a time for self-reflection / Bonnie S. Bostrom
with Barbara Reider.
      p. cm.
  Includes bibliographical references.
  ISBN 0-944031-28-5 (alk. paper)
  1. Retirement—Psychological aspects. 2. Retired women—United
States—Psychology. 3. Self-help techniques. I. Reider, Barbara. II. Title.

  HQ1062.B57 2006
  646.7'9082—dc22

                              2006019279

Editing and book design by Dianne Schilling
Cover design by Miggs Burroughs
Printing by R.R. Donnelley
Printed in the USA

This book is dedicated to our daughters, those we gave birth to and those that life has given us through special grace:

Barbara Martin
Heather Reider
Janet Gray
Michelle Reider
Kim Sutton
Anna Wolfe

and to the women who gave us their stories, who shared their fears, tears, dreams and dragons, and who by doing so have enriched us all by great measure. Thank you.

| | |
|---|---|
| Jill Adams | Carolyn Jernigan |
| Silvia Almeida | JonLee Joseph |
| Bettye Bobroff | Kylee Kidder |
| Myra Blackburn | Jenny Lemire |
| Roslyn de Jesus Cann | Carol McDermott |
| Manon Chabonneau | Barbara Martin |
| Carla Christianson | Lori Miller |
| Paula Clayton | Eleanor Minik |
| Jean Collins | Katherine Moore |
| Phyllis Constan | Betty Nehemias |
| Sylvia Cooke | Phyllis Nye |
| Kate Fallon | Martha Perry |
| Jean Farrell | Georgeann Raco |
| Ellen Feldman | Ann Ragsdale |
| Christine Golden | Beverly Saltz |
| Malissa Haslam | Marilyn Sapsford |
| Rita Herbert | Paula Schandel |
| Virginia Heyler | Dovie St. Peters |
| Carol Hoffman | Felicite Woods |
| Donna Holm | |

# Acknowledgments

I want to acknowledge my writing partner Barbara Reider. She has encouraged me throughout the endeavor and was the reader to whom I wrote; the first responder, and the person who understands most deeply the transformative change that can happen in the process of leaving one's career.

Sunamita Lim took the first draft of the book, guided me through the process of completely revamping it, and helped me create a book proposal that captured the attention of my publisher, Barbara Levine, of Aslan Publishing.

Barbara Levine's belief in the efficacy of this book, and the message that it holds for women who are and will be facing the challenges of retirement, has carried it to completion.

Every writer hopes for a great editor, someone who takes what you have and polishes the rough stone to diamond brightness. If this book shines it is due in large part to my editor, Dianne Schilling.

Special thanks to Miggs Burroughs for his artistry and expertise. He created a cover that is evocative and beautiful at the same time.

Although I dedicated this book to my daughter, Barbara, I could not have written it without the men in my life—son Bobby Martin, who acts as my personal advisor, stepson Kiva Bitar, who keeps me up on politics, and beloved husband Jim Bostrom, who first diagnosed me with "empty desk syndrome" and who has witnessed my journey from the "darkened mirror" to the "spirit within."

—Bonnie S. Bostrom
June, 2006

# Foreword

Professional equality with men, freedom and choice consti-tuted the dominant discourse of women's liberation in the 70s and 80s. This was the terrain on which the women in this book forged and furthered their careers. It is the same ground of conscious-ness—this expectation of equal opportunity—into which I had the luxury of being born. I am a daughter of the generation of women who offer their stories between these pages. Listening to the inti-mate voices of my foremothers as they reflect on the triumphs and tragedies of retirement is an eye-opening experience. Retirement is a life stage that we, as a society, are just beginning to imprint on the developmental map of women's psychology.

The sheer demographic power of the boomer generation is calling us to attend to this life passage with a deeper awareness. In particular, with a critical mass of women who have spent the bet-ter part of their lives in the workforce now coming of retirement age, we are asking new questions about women's work and women's worth. A conversation is beginning that extends beyond the public-private sphere dichotomy and requires an integral view of women's lives.

The perennial questions of power and meaning, and the relationship between the two, are a recursive pattern that figures prominently in each woman's story. Power is reasserted, or refigured, and sometimes redefined, but cannot go unaddressed. Meaning is lost, or refashioned, and sometimes forged anew, but cannot be taken for granted. Money and power, generally perceived as aspects of a man's world, are brought to the fore in this book, because they are central to the lives of women. As women explore these issues in their narratives, we begin to ask new questions and perceive new patterns. One pattern that connects these women's individual experiences—inquiry into what gives us a sense of power and what gives our lives meaning—is as instructive to women in retirement as it is to women approaching retirement. Moreover, this text is as relevant for women in the full stride of their professional lives as it is for any woman who is questioning her life priorities.

Many women who have lived out what psychiatrist Jean Shinoda Bolen coined the "Athena" superwoman archetype let down their guard on these pages as they reflect on the gains and losses of stepping into the public domain alongside men. As they leave that domain and enter into retirement, we learn that it is a time to reorient to and reclaim those tasks of the heart, soul and spirit that were sometimes traded or minimized in the bargain. These rich and varied stories, guided by Bonnie Bostrom's poetic eye and lyrical craft, reveal the soft underbelly of Athena. What does the famed warrior have to say as she lays down her breast plate by her side, steps out of the public gaze and moves beyond the cultural proving ground?

We read on these pages the true confessions of women who achieved unprecedented success in the outer forms of social and economic power. Against the backdrop of their accomplishments, it is instructive to read about what these women experience as a life-in-the-shadows as they approach, or find themselves thrust into, retirement. For some women, retirement is a time of transformation. For others, it is a tumultuous time spent translating established priorities into a new context. All of the women who share their stories experience a common initiation: a core dimension of self relegated to the shadows. What does a woman who, by all outward appearances, "has it all" identify as the unlived life? And how does Athena then emerge out of the shadows and claim the life yet to live?

In these stories of retirement recovery, we hear tones of an inward call to a different calibration of power that neither waxes nor wanes—a power that abides within each woman. This call is potent. It is a call to create, to risk a deeper order of love and to clarify that which is essential: to know oneself. The results of that self-knowing are as varied as the contributors, but the constant thread of self-reflection is the path. Some ease into a part-time work commitment, move to a new community or embark on international travel. Others tend the garden of their soul, one seedling at a time or one painting at a time. One or two grieve the death of a beloved life partner and begin anew as single women. And many tend the community through volunteer contributions.

As a practicing psychotherapist, the art and science of helping people to vision and craft a life worth living is my daily work. The most difficult steps in the process of psychotherapy are the first ones: acknowledging a difficulty, reaching out for support, unveiling both the struggle and the strengths one harbors to address that struggle. Just knowing you are not alone in a particular life transition is in itself monumental.

Bostrom begins to validate the developmental dimension of women in retirement by rendering that dimension visible and audible without diminishing its diverse faces. In these respects, this book is an invaluable reference for assisting women to acknowledge the largely uncharted twists and turns of retirement, and to begin that journey. It gently holds up a mirror to this emerging self so that those approaching or already immersed in the fire of this transformation will perceive themselves more clearly in it, and appreciate more deeply the woman they see.

—Willow Pearson, MA, LPC, Mt-BC
    Lionessroars Therapeutic Arts & Integral Psychotherapy Center
    Integral Institute
    Boulder, Colorado

# Contents

**Introduction** . . . . . . . . . . . . . . . . . . . . . . . . . . . . . . xv

1   **The Darkened Mirror**
    The Loss of Professional Identity . . . . . . . . . . . . . . . . . . . .1

2   **Rose-Tinted Glass**
    Naive Notions of Retirement Nirvana . . . . . . . . . . . . . .11

3   **Images of Power**
    Leaving the Career Perks Behind . . . . . . . . . . . . . . . . 21

4   **When the Mirror Breaks**
    The Painful Reality of Forced Retirement . . . . . . . . . . . 31

5   **Disrobing Before the Mirror**
    Aging in a Society Dedicated to Youth . . . . . . . . . . . . . 37

6   **Dragons in the Mirror**
    Dealing with Post-Retirement Depression . . . . . . . . . . . 47

7   **Seeking a New Reflection**
    Accounts of Successful Transitions . . . . . . . . . . . . . . . . 63

8   **Dusting Off the Mirror of Dreams**
    Taking Risks and Fulfilling Lifelong Aspirations . . . . . . . 77

9   **A Closer Look**
    Self-reflection, Preparation and Planning . . . . . . . . . . . 101

10  **Uncovering the Mirror**
    Discovering the Spirit Within . . . . . . . . . . . . . . . . . . . .111

    **References** . . . . . . . . . . . . . . . . . . . . . . . . . . . . . .120

    **Self-Help Exercises** . . . . . . . . . . . . . . . . . . . . . . . . .121

    **About the Authors** . . . . . . . . . . . . . . . . . . . . . . . . .138

# Contributor Listings

Jill Adams . . . . . . . . . . . . . . . . . . . . . . . . . . . . . . . . . . . . . . . . . 17
Silvia Almeida . . . . . . . . . . . . . . . . . . . . . . . . . . . . . . . . . . . . . . .32
Bettye Bobroff . . . . . . . . . . . . . . . . . . . . . . . . . . . . . . . . . . . . . 105
Myra Blackburn . . . . . . . . . . . . . . . . . . . . . . . . . . . . . . . . . . . . . 72
Bonnie Bostrom . . . . . . . . . . . . . . . . . . . 5, 25, 41, 45, 50, 52, 57, 59, 83, 102
Roslyn de Jesus Cann . . . . . . . . . . . . . . . . . . . . . . . . . . . . . . . . . . . 6
Manon Chabonneau . . . . . . . . . . . . . . . . . . . . . . . . . . . . . . . . . . . .94
Carla Christianson . . . . . . . . . . . . . . . . . . . . . . . . . . . . . . . . . . . . .33
Paula Clayton . . . . . . . . . . . . . . . . . . . . . . . . . . . . . . . . . . . . . . 92
Jean Collins . . . . . . . . . . . . . . . . . . . . . . . . . . . . . . . . . . . . . 58, 84
Phyllis Constan . . . . . . . . . . . . . . . . . . . . . . . . . . . . . . . . . . . 97, 99
Sylvia Cooke . . . . . . . . . . . . . . . . . . . . . . . . . . . . . . . . . . . . . . .96
Kate Fallon . . . . . . . . . . . . . . . . . . . . . . . . . . . . . . . . . . . . . . . .18
Jean Farrell . . . . . . . . . . . . . . . . . . . . . . . . . . . . . . . . . . . . . . . 24
Ellen Feldman . . . . . . . . . . . . . . . . . . . . . . . . . . . . . . . . . . . . . .90
Christine Golden . . . . . . . . . . . . . . . . . . . . . . . . . . . . . . . . . . . . .15
Malissa Haslam . . . . . . . . . . . . . . . . . . . . . . . . . . . . . . . . . . . . .112
Rita Herbert . . . . . . . . . . . . . . . . . . . . . . . . . . . . . . . . . . . . . . .44
Virginia Heyler . . . . . . . . . . . . . . . . . . . . . . . . . . . . . . . . . . . . . 94
Carol Hoffman . . . . . . . . . . . . . . . . . . . . . . . . . . . . . . . . . . . 54, 83
Donna Holm . . . . . . . . . . . . . . . . . . . . . . . . . . . . . . . . . . . . . . .27
Carolyn Jernigan . . . . . . . . . . . . . . . . . . . . . . . . . . . . . . . . . . . . 80
JonLee Joseph . . . . . . . . . . . . . . . . . . . . . . . . . . . . . . . . . . . 81, 84
Kylee Kidder . . . . . . . . . . . . . . . . . . . . . . . . . . . . . . . . . . . . . . 12
Jenny Lemire . . . . . . . . . . . . . . . . . . . . . . . . . . . . . . . . . . . . . .117
Carol McDermott . . . . . . . . . . . . . . . . . . . . . . . . . . . . . . . . . . 40, 52
Barbara Martin . . . . . . . . . . . . . . . . . . . . . . . . . . . . . . . . . . . . . .11
Lori Miller . . . . . . . . . . . . . . . . . . . . . . . . . . . . . . . . . . . . . . . .14
Eleanor Minik . . . . . . . . . . . . . . . . . . . . . . . . . . . . . . . . . . . . . . 43
Katherine Moore . . . . . . . . . . . . . . . . . . . . . . . . . . . . . . . . . . 39, 115
Betty Nehemias . . . . . . . . . . . . . . . . . . . . . . . . . . . . . . . . . . . . . 8
Phyllis Nye . . . . . . . . . . . . . . . . . . . . . . . . . . . . . . . . . . . . . . . 65
Martha Perry . . . . . . . . . . . . . . . . . . . . . . . . . . . . . . . . . . . . . . .89
Georgeann Raco . . . . . . . . . . . . . . . . . . . . . . . . . . . . . . . . . . . . .35
Ann Ragsdale . . . . . . . . . . . . . . . . . . . . . . . . . . . . . . . . . . . . . . 76
Barbara Reider . . . . . . . . . . . . . . . . . . . 22, 29, 44, 47, 51, 63, 69, 107
Beverly Saltz . . . . . . . . . . . . . . . . . . . . . . . . . . . . . . . . . . . . . . .67
Marilyn Sapsford . . . . . . . . . . . . . . . . . . . . . . . . . . . . . . . . . . . . 77
Paula Schandel . . . . . . . . . . . . . . . . . . . . . . . . . . . . . . . . . . . . . 13
Dovie St. Peters . . . . . . . . . . . . . . . . . . . . . . . . . . . . . . . . . . . . .31
Felicite Woods . . . . . . . . . . . . . . . . . . . . . . . . . . . . . . . . . . . 23, 105

# Introduction

This book is written for women who are in transition from the world of work to the phase of life we call "retirement." It is for women who want to explore what it means to be themselves in new ways, or who feel they are losing their way and need some signposts in this new territory. Perhaps knowing that thousands of women are making this journey together will encourage those who feel unnecessarily isolated.

This year (2006), some 78 million baby boomers will turn 60, and the next 20 years will see the number of retirees climb to approximately 115 million. This means that millions of women will leave the workplace, either by choice or obligation. It is an extraordinary time in history and represents great change for the world and for women.

Women have found themselves before the mirror of radical change many times throughout history and within the contextual frames of their own lives. Here, we follow in the steps of 41 separate women as they enter into or contemplate the particularly daunting changes wrought by retirement. We begin this collective journey standing before a darkened mirror—a mirror filled with mystery, with subtle and shadowy images—and progress through stages of transformation until we are ready at last to uncover the mirror and embrace the the part of ourselves that has survived the journey—the spirit within.

*Women Facing Retirement* was born out of depression—mine and that of my writing partner, Barbara Reider. During a conversation, Barbara and I, both recently retired, realized that we were experiencing very similar feelings. We quickly concluded that, rather than instantly conferring joyful freedom, the step of retiring often ushered in a period of profound loss and mourning. This seemed to us a phenomenon worth exploring. Admitting to each other that we were having difficulty with retirement proved so helpful, we immediately launched the project that led to this book.

Barbara and I began by collecting stories from women we knew. Soon we were receiving calls from women who heard about our project and wanted to talk about their experiences. The information coalesced very quickly as word of mouth spread across the country. Women referred their friends, or people they knew of, who were going through difficult times. And so the stories came to us. We did not have to search. We developed friendships with many of the women whose stories we gathered; others we have never met. Many stories are just as they were sent to us; others were transcribed from interviews—they talked while we wrote.

We interviewed women who have dealt with what I call the "empty desk syndrome" with great ease. Their stories encourage and inspire us. We also have stories from women just beginning to think about retirement and from a few who are years away from retirement and view it in remote and idealistic terms. Finally, a significant number of the women we interviewed were despondent and confused. They expressed deep anger and described numbing depression, much as Barbara and I experienced.

We are grateful to have had the opportunity to learn from the women we interviewed. We are tremendously indebted to them and honored that they agreed to share their stories and lives in this book. We present the stories of these wonderful women, along with our own, in the hope that readers will be encouraged and will know that they are not alone.

—Bonnie S. Bostrom
June, 2006

# The Darkened Mirror
## The Loss of Professional Identity

*The Talmud teaches that when someone dies the mirrors are covered. This ritual has a two-fold purpose. It reminds the living that this is a time for self-reflection, for answering the question: "Who am I without the dead?" A second, mystical dimension has to do with the seven days during which the soul leaves the body. If the mirror were left uncovered, the transcending soul might look into the mirror and, failing to see the self, find the process of leaving the body more difficult. The mirror would tempt the soul back into the material world to look for itself. The soul must find the incorporeal self, which has no physical image. Covering the mirror symbolizes the death experience when one's reflection cannot be seen.*
*—Interpretation from the Talmud*

When retirement thrusts us before the mirror of radical change, we cannot readily see where we are. We know what our experience has been up to that point and long to see the familiar past reflected back to us. We had a lock on reality—how it looked to us, and how we assumed it looked to others. Then reality changed.

We can look around and see the externals that change has wrought, but we cannot see the intangibles—our feelings about the change. We know what we look like, where we live, what our favorite book is, but we don't know how to decipher the new feelings that arrive when our world morphs from its familiar shape, starts to blur out, and we descend into darkness.

The self senses this change as a loss, as a death of sorts, and yet knows that it is still alive and feeling pain. No longer able to depend upon old familiar signposts in the exterior world of work, the self must turn inward to understand the meaning of the experience.

The mirror is a metaphor for how we see ourselves. The darkened mirror, representing this drastic change, gives back no light, no easily understood image. We don't know ourselves. We stand in a new place. That which is on the other side of the mirror is lost to us, unattainable, perhaps no longer exists. We are in a painful transition between the old and the new, and so we turn from the mirror and begin the task of recovery, the journey into healing and wholeness.

The darkened mirror is a metaphor for women going through the radical change that retirement heralds. That which occludes the reflected image causes refractions and distortions, which in turn cause pain.

Our pain usually results from thoughts we have about ourselves. We think that we are now old, that we are no longer useful, that we don't know who we are, what to do, or what we will become. The mirror is before us. We know that we must face it and find a new image of ourselves. Owning the darkness is not easy.

Mirrors call to women all their lives. We concern ourselves with how we look to others, how we seem to ourselves, and what we find reflected back to us from the relationships we create. This book focuses on the relationship women have with work and the transition that occurs when we retire.

When we work, who we are is reflected back to us from the relationships we establish in the workplace. If we are the secretary, or have a secretary; if we are the boss, or have a boss—the environment is relational.

Women have a unique theory of relativity and go about the physics of life connecting the invisible dots of a picture that only we can see. We construct ourselves, in part, from the connections we have created in our careers. The career doesn't really stand alone; it is an amalgam of constructed connections that has at its base the consistency of emotional engagement.

When we stand before the mirror of retirement, we begin relinquishing many of these emotional bonds. The transition can be difficult.

Millions of us have reached retirement age. We are a generation of women at ease with power, decision making, and leadership. We set our sights on the corporate world and we proved that we could be entrepreneurs, own businesses, make money, and have success. We became doctors, lawyers, merchants, and, yes, Indian chiefs. We reached for the golden ring, had it reset with diamonds and slipped it on comfortably. We wielded power in new ways, and both men and other women learned from us because we brought great value to society.

Women set precedents by bringing to the workplace more open and inclusive styles of planning and decision-making. Now that we are leaving work by the millions, we face the exciting prospect of bringing to society new ways of being in the world. We can become activists, formulating new knowledge and wisdom. We have a complex task: to ride the rapids of radical change in our own lives and to find calm waters where we can rest and gear up for the remainder of the journey.

In the workplace we skidded from ocean to shore like high-tide surfers, like fish in the right water. We lost sight of the shore that was ourselves and the ocean that was work and submerged ourselves in the wonderful water of work. Yes, that's how we were in our jobs. Now, we stand before the mirror and say goodbye to the careers that defined us. It's a tough business, facing the "empty desk syndrome."

We are emotionally engaged when we fall in love, when we give birth, and when we say goodbye to our kindergartner on the first day of school. We bury our dead and nourish the funeral party with food that we have made ourselves—we carry on. We operate in, and through, the emotional realm as we build constructs that become companies, hard working teams, successful businesses and excellent service organizations. When it comes time to extract ourselves from the constructs we have spent our lives creating, we sometimes lose ourselves.

We sit before the desk for the last time and begin to empty the drawers. As we remove those final papers, the bits and pieces of ourselves we had stored away in the dark recesses of our desks, we may reflect on who we are and the power we wield.

The power to create, to construct realities, and to prosper from our creations epitomizes the human spirit. Transforming chaos into order gives us a great feeling of joy and deep closure. What woman isn't delighted when it all comes together the way she planned it and everybody benefits? We can stand before that mirror in the board room when we report that the project came in under budget. When our students walk across the stage and accept diplomas, we smile into the mirror knowing our guidance got them there. The BMW, the Mercedes, the Lexus, or just new tires on the Honda Accord—we did it. We bask in our reflection in the rearview mirror as we drive to work in the car we bought.

Yes, we can buy things, lots of things. We can take courses with celebrities to make us even better at what we do. We smile into a compact mirror as we get ready to walk on stage to give the commencement address at our favorite university. It's fun to get into a limo and drive to the Berkshires for a week at Canyon Ranch when we're on the East Coast, and when we're in California the mud baths of Calistoga make it all worthwhile. Money is lovely. It can even buy a better reflection in the vanity mirror. A little tuck, some bruising, and we are back at work reflecting health and vitality, the rested look.

What about when we get tired inside? Where is the magic potion for the knees and feet that have carried the nurse from floor to floor for 30 years, or the bookkeeper who can't stand the thought of one more spreadsheet? What if we become more concerned about our own bottom line falling than that of the company we're running? We start thinking about retirement and how wonderful it will be.

"I won't have to…" and we finish the sentence with whatever task we are sick and tired of doing. Like getting up in the morning and having to face the mirror that asks, "How long are you going to do this?" Then we start thinking about letting go and get so scared that we turn the lights out in the mirror and hurry to work.

 When I resigned from my last job, I had no preparation for what came after. I had some fantasies about relaxation and recreation, about leisure and the luxury of time, and vague notions about freedom. "Freedom from" was fairly clear in my mind. I would have freedom from the relentless ritual of being in service, answering the call to responsibility and being dependable. I would have freedom from my office, my day-planner and the constant barrage of telephone calls, meetings and agendas. "Freedom to" was an empty set—the "x" in a strange equation of novelty and anticipation mixed with apprehension. I had some ideas, quite abstract, about what I might do, but my focus was directed toward that freedom. I had no inkling of a future. I was so caught up in letting go of the present as embodied in my career that I forgot to picture myself in a different future. A future without a career! My mind could not compute the solution to an equation for which I had no experience in my adult life. I had always been working and I didn't have a clue about not working."

—*Bonnie S. Bostrom, M.A., former Chief of Education, Mashantucket Pequot Tribal Nation*

We not only leave work and the relationships that sustained us there, we also leave cities and states behind. It isn't easy to make ourselves anew, or to find a place within a new environment. It is hard just to leave work in the first place, but if you have to leave the area where you have invested your time and energy, where you have played, dreamed, and achieved, the trauma can be multiplied exponentially.

 After working in public and community health education for twenty years and enjoying the experience, I was reluctant to retire. My colleagues were getting younger and the demands greater. The closer I drew to the planned time to submit my resignation, the more nervous and anxious I became. I felt so comfortable and gratified in my work. I asked myself, "Will I ever again have the opportunity to meet such provocative challenges?" I loved my last six years helping disenfranchised youth achieve interdependence and self-worth.

My husband left his position as a hospital administrator just weeks before my departure, which meant we would be making a great change at the same time. I remember while we were preparing to leave for Florida, I visited my old job on several occasions and truly faced reality when a manager whom I knew well and had an excellent rapport with exclaimed, "What are you doing here?" I felt strange and alienated. I began to realize... "Well Roz, when it's over, it's over. Wake up and get in touch with reality!"

I felt a mixture of curiosity about Florida and strong emotional bonding with New York City, my home. I began to feel frightened. What does a workaholic do to begin adjusting to a new environment and lifestyle? A true dilemma, I thought, but I also remembered my sense of optimism and my tenacity, two survival skills clearly modeled by my parents.

Upon arriving in Florida, I had no idea I would be so tense and reflective, always thinking about New York, missing my family and friends and not giving Florida a chance. Adding to my difficulty in acclimating was the matter of driving. In New York I took public transportation most of the time, rarely rode the highways. I never had a thought about transportation prior to moving to Florida. In order to get around I had to learn to drive long distances. My husband reminded me not to lean on him. If I wanted to work part time, as planned, I had to get the confidence to drive regularly and for many miles.

I realized I had been resisting the change and was psychologically connected to the north. I decided that I was the only person able to create my own emotional, spiritual, and social sense of inner peace, so I made up my mind to perceive and believe that Florida was my new home and that I was here to stay.

It has taken me almost three years to adjust to the new Florida "culture." I'm meeting new people constantly, enjoying many cultural events, working part time as a mentor-educator and finding it gratifying. The reluctant retiree is no longer reluctant; I'm enjoying the process and recognizing the value and pride in being a senior adult still learning and growing and eager to meet new challenges as long as I live.

—*Roslyn De Jesus Cann, former Community Health Education Specialist, Department of Health, City of New York*

As we learn to adapt to external geographic change and daily routine change, another dimension begins to open up to us—the dimension of inner life. The usual thoughts we used to have are inappropriate in our new settings. New routines can be confusing, as Roslyn found when she was faced with something as seemingly innocuous as transportation. The simple acts we once took for granted are not there to comfort us, to give us a sense of the ordinary and familiar. Other actions must be taken, new thoughts occur. We are out of familiar territory and it can be very troubling, even debilitating.

We don't always get the dreams we plan for and treasure. Our paths to those dreams are sometimes beset with great calamity, burdens that grind away at us until, when we look to see what is left, we find the essential strength to carry on.

Jack and I met in 1943 at a church social. Jack was stationed in England with the U.S. Army and I was a Red Cross volunteer—one of the hostesses for the evening. We met again in 1945 when he returned to England for some R&R after being wounded in France. Over the years we corresponded frequently and were married in Canada in 1947.

Married life was interesting. Jack was at Brookhaven National Laboratory on Long Island and the University of Michigan in Ann Arbor, where he taught graduate physics and worked at the fission products lab. As a result of these experiences Jack and the lab director gave lectures at Oxford (I was more than happy to accompany him). Jack, still with the Atomic Energy Commission, was invited to the United Nations in Geneva to write the World Standard on Radiation protection. His doctoral thesis was on the effect of radiation on humans resulting from the atomic bomb. During this time he also visited the IAEA in Vienna. Upon returning to the United States, Jack joined the Nuclear Regulatory Commission. The Mexican government invited Jack to assist with nuclear energy, which he did. They invited him to remain permanently, but he returned to the United States and stayed with the Nuclear Regulatory Commission until his retirement in 1984.

When Jack and I retired in 1984 we started to plan a special dream: to walk together from Lands End at the Southwest tip of England to John of Groats at the Northeast tip of Scotland. We belonged to a hiking club and walked together everywhere. It was a beautiful goal, and we talked about how long it would take; we figured from two to three months. We imagined where we would stop on the way and what we would take with us. It was great fun planning our trip.

In 1986 Jack had his first stroke. I was in shock. I could not accept that this healthy, robust man who walked three miles a day, played tennis regularly, hiked each weekend and danced, who had never smoked, drank very little, ate in moderation and had a happy, grateful heart, could be stricken that way. Before we could adjust to the first stroke, while Jack was at the National Institute of Health as a patient, he had the second stroke, much more debilitating than the first.

I was in denial and spent the first two years frantically trying everything I could find to cure him, to make him well, to stop the process that was robbing him of his life, his identity. I would hear of a nutritionist or a neurologist or a lymphologist. I would take him from doctor to doctor and from institute to clinic, all to no avail. It was so wrong, it seemed so unfair. He was always sensible about exercise and diet. At one time he said," I'm so sorry this happened. It's not fair you should go through this." I would have gone through anything for Jack.

I cared for him at home for ten years. As time went by he lost his ability to communicate or concentrate, but he could walk. That was all he could do and he wanted to walk incessantly. I'm sure it gave him a sense of purpose and control, something he had in no other aspect of his life. But sometimes I would awaken in the night and know that he had gone out walking. I would have to call the police to help find him and bring him home. He was sometimes walking as many as twenty-five miles a day and I could not keep up with him. I hired a person to walk with him, but that turned unpleasant, as the companion was proselytizing Jack every step of the way.

Once, and only once, in our entire life did I ever hear Jack say anything that could be construed as non-acceptance of his situation. When he was constrained from walking, he asked, "Is it asking too much to be allowed to walk?" That broke my heart.

I had to face reality when I realized how much weight I had lost. I weighed only 98 pounds. My children helped to convince me that Jack needed to be in an environment where he could be cared for, and so we moved him to an assisted living home nearby. He has been there now for five years and I go every day to feed him his dinner and to sit with him and tell him the events of my day. And I have a lot to tell. When we moved to Florida twelve years ago, there was a center near our home, the Life Forces Research Foundation, and I began to volunteer there. The "dome" (the foundation was in a huge geodesic dome) provided a great array of consciousness-raising activities. I became the director after a time.

Groups of people at the center were studying meditation, nutrition, healing modalities and Feldenkrais. We had Sunday services, conferences, guest speakers and "dances of universal peace." It was wonderful, but the center has now closed. I have learned that if I can look with kindness at what is, that's truly enough. The negative events that happened to me have been catalysts for positive, creative outcomes in my life.

I am still dancing. We have a weekly class in international folk dancing, and I usually walk three miles a day and swim twice. I also very much enjoy my volunteer work with those who are housebound and, of course, the joy of friendships. Happiness is a habit, one we all need to cultivate in retirement.

I sit with Jack and sometimes I dream. I dream that we are walking together. I have my special walking boots on and he is carrying the heavier pack. We are heading out toward the early sunrise. We are walking hand in hand in a northeasterly direction toward John of Groats.

—*Betty Nehemias, Dancer, Educator*

We stand before the mirror of memory and take comfort from our dreams. Then we turn back to what is real and move through the pain of transition. Transition is our journey.

# Rose-Tinted Glass
## Naïve Notions of Retirement Nirvana

Looking back, many of us may recall our naïve notions of what we thought retirement would be. Back then we probably had on the same rose-colored glasses that women half our age may be wearing today. We had no handle on what retirement would bring, what adventures might unfold. But we probably had strong hopes and dreams.

Young women, early in their careers, with babies and mortgages and never enough sleep, dream of retirement as a place of rest and recuperation. They secure themselves in the present by holding on to the sweet dream of how it will be when they no longer are pulled in every direction at once.

 What will retirement look like? I'm not sure, but I have a fairly good idea of what it *won't* be like. Each morning, Monday through Friday, I will not get up at five in order to avoid traffic getting into town. When it snows, I will not ask my husband to plow the driveway so that I can slip and slide my way to work. I will not have to call my kids' babysitter to tell her I'm running late again, and could she please give them a snack to tide them over until I can get home and fix dinner. And, most certainly, retirement will mean that never again will I ever have to feel guilty about turning off the snooze alarm more than once.

When I retire, which will be in about twenty years (Hey I'm more than halfway there), I would first like to take a trip to shake off the working woman's blues. Next, I would love to…start working again. Yes, I am already looking at the career possibilities that retirement surely will bring. Shall I start my own children's theater? Or will I open up a daycare center? Maybe by then I'll switch gears and get out of teaching. Perhaps I can help my husband run his business unless he retires before me, in which case he can help me run mine. The wonderful feeling about retirement is that it is so open-ended. The possibilities can change with the weather, since each day you are given the time and opportunity to make new decisions about the future, like, "What kind of socks do I want to wear today?" or, "Shall I get dressed and go out, or hang around in this bathrobe and slippers until noon?" This is what I look forward to about retirement.

—*Barbara Martin, Teacher*

Some women organize their lives so there will be a seamless transition from their chosen work to the retirement years. They focus early on what might work for them.

 In one month I'll be twenty-three. "I am…" is such a definitive beginning, like who you are is what you do. Even though I'm not in school, I think of myself as a student. I work as a waitress, but "I am" a writer and I don't think you can ever retire from being a writer.

I always say that the reason I have such a bad work ethic is my dad was retired when I was born, so there was no role model for me. My mother died when I was quite young.

I went away to Smith College because it was very far from my Arizona home and I felt that drastic change would give me strength to survive. The coldness of the people and the weather proved too much for an Arizona girl, so now I am living in New Orleans.

I hope that during the years I'm working I don't allow work to take over my life, that I continue to do the things I like to do. It's important that I find creative ways to enrich my life so that I will keep learning. No matter what profession I go into, I want to start doing things that I can continue doing when I retire. I don't want to start over when I retire. I want to continue developing creatively all my life.

I am more fearful about finding my life's profession than I am about retiring. I want to love what I do, but it is hard to find people who love their work. I'd like to find a profession that I can do my whole life, so that work and retirement will be one continuous experience, not broken up in different segments.

—*Kylee Kidder, Writer*

Women frequently find themselves going through divorce at a time when their careers have taken on greater importance. Often they are raising a family and have to reconstruct their lives while staying strong and centered for their children. Work can provide women with needed engagement during a time of great upheaval.

 Retirement doesn't have much meaning to me, because I don't see myself in formal retirement for at least another thirty years, if that. I am fifty-one years old right now. When my husband of eighteen years left me eleven years ago, I had no idea what was down the road for me. That was my first retirement. I had to retire from being a wife, having a complete family. I had to resign from my dreams of a particular future.

Retiring from dreams. That's the hard part of change. We don't think about that when we get married or start a career. My dreams were going in a certain direction. It wasn't until my mate turned off the path that I saw those dreams for what they really were: assumptions. I had assumed a future and when that future wasn't possible, I had to assume another one.

Now, after years of being on my own and raising two wonderful children to the point of college and beyond, I have a much different vision for myself, but it is just a vision and can change at the drop of a hat. I envision my future as a therapist facilitating positive change in the bodies, minds and spirits of those I treat. I was a dental hygienist for thirty years, but during the past fifteen I have trained and become proficient in several massage and healing modalities. I have observed the power of these techniques to transform and heal others, as well as myself. I am getting ready to pursue my bodywork practice with more vigor and see where it takes me. I am going to open my own business.

I enjoy this work immensely and feel no yearning to retire from it as long as I am helping others and nourishing myself through its practice. I feel empowered to finally do the work I find most rewarding, and I will do it for as long as I wish, on my own terms, and will bring my own spiritual evolution into my work. I have retired from a former life and that experience will sustain me forever. If life takes a left turn off the present path, I'll just dream a different future."

—*Paula Schandel, Dental Hygienist and Advanced Bodyworker, Ormond Beach, Florida*

When we are already doing something we love, it isn't difficult to plot out the future if we can take our present occupation along with us. Craftswomen and successful artists seem to view retirement as an opportunity to expand their creativity, do more of what they are already doing successfully.

 It's hard to pinpoint what I am going to do when I retire, but I would like it to involve art and craft shows with my husband. I'm also interested in displaying and selling our art on the Internet and in galleries, book stores and coffee houses. We are currently preparing to begin shows within the next two years.

It would be great to travel, see grandbabies, friends and family, and do a show to pay for the trip. What could be better than that?

I also think it's important to grow spiritually during retirement, and having an abundance of time will help this happen. It seems that as I get older I want to go deeper within myself.

I am very at home with Native American beliefs. My husband and I have been blessed with a wonderful spiritual community. We attend Native American workshops that are giving us the tools for self-healing. I think this time of life is for healing the past in order to enjoy the present. The future is an adventure. If you are at peace with yourself, most of the fears leave and you find excitement in the years ahead. Heck, people can do just about anything they want. I think that what is crucial is to do something!

My husband and I just moved to fifteen acres of land in the foothills of the Rocky Mountains where we grow flowers and vegetables in the summer. Gardening makes us both very happy. Fifteen acres allows us to have plenty of projects. That's what we like. The only real fear I have is of being left alone without my beautiful partner. It would be hard, I know, but I hope I would have the courage to do all the things I love to do and be open to life and to what Spirit would have me do. Life is great. It's a blessing to be breathing. I know one thing—I would never be one to waste it.

—*Lori Miller, Artist and Co-owner, The Gourd Lady and Me,*
*Trinidad, Colorado*

For many, the retirement years are distant, vague and mysterious. Women who are looking forward to the time when they will leave work approach it with different emotions, plans, and expectations. They look for themes and threads of meaning while searching for what they want in their lives.

I plan to retire within five or six years, ten at the most, but lots of days I wonder why I don't retire now so I can do the things I want to do. When I do retire, I want to take art classes. In fact, I intend to sign up for a class soon. I don't want to wait until I retire.

I have a new appreciation for travel. I recently moved after having lived in the same state all my life and in the same house for the past twenty-six years. I have traveled to Japan and Germany, but I will look differently at travel now.

Moving caused a greater openness in me. I think that now I feel more connected to people, whether I know them or not. I'm more open and have a greater ability to just start talking to people and quickly form genuine bonds. I am anxious to travel and discover if the experience really will be different.

Work caused me to neglect my health and my body. I plan to get into shape—healthy diet, walking, biking. I'm going to put some energy into this, sharpen the saw so to speak. Mine is more than a little rusty. I really look forward to this aspect of retirement.

I want to be involved in the community through volunteer work, maybe in a children's hospital. I'd also like to get back into doing some theater. Being a school principal kept me from pursuing theater in the way I would have liked. My role in the community inhibited me from fully expressing myself. When I retire, I believe I will have more freedom. I could shave my head, go without makeup, not worry about my "public image." There is a wildness in me that I've had to tone down a lot, being a principal. Part of me wonders, though, if I will really do these things when I retire—if I have the guts.

Sometimes I imagine what a day of retirement would be like. I would take my time getting up in the morning, never looking at a clock. I would pad around, maybe do some yoga. I'd have a studio where I could paint. Then perhaps brunch with friends, volunteer work and out to dinner with more friends. Or I might stay home and watch a video, keep a journal, go to the theater.

I see a slow pace, without the onus of having tasks to do. Just relax, plan a trip. Now I don't even have the energy to phone friends and family. I'm on the phone at work so much.

Unlike most of my divorced friends, I do not see myself with a partner. Their talk about retiring is around finding a man. If it happens, finding a partner will occur naturally, not because I'm planning for it.

I have only one concern: that I'll wait too long to retire. I ask myself, "Why don't you just do it?" My fear is tied to money. I have a two-person income for only one person. I have already retired once and receive an excellent retirement. My present salary is good. I enjoy having money and I'm holding back because I can do things now that I could never do before.

I do recognize that my identity is tied to being the principal of a school. I am introduced as the principal, not as myself, and am wondering if I will miss it more than I realize. It may have an effect on me that I haven't anticipated. Still, I'm looking forward to finding out who I am twenty-four hours a day.

What if I retire and I do the art and it doesn't work? I have trepidation, but in a good way. My heart beats a little faster when I think about retiring. I'm starting to watch people who are already retired, seeing how they fill their days. I'm getting ideas, seeing different models. Attitude seems to be the key.

I bought a retirement planner a few years ago, and it was mostly about money. There was something about planning your time and the pitfalls of not planning, but I don't think it's going to be any problem for me. I think I'll just sail.

My feeling is that I'll be active—maybe join Rotary to get connected. There are a lot of organizations I can get involved in. Many educators stay connected to the schools in some way, or serve as consultants. I might consider that. On the other hand, I've been in school all my life.

I have a rich interior life and as I look around me I see people focused on a particular philosophy or some kind of spiritual practice. I want to become more structured in my beliefs. Sometimes I feel sucked away from my interior life, pulled away by my job. Sometimes I go for days and forget the beauty and spirit in everything around me. I want to be more coherent about spiritual practice, and this ties in with my desire to produce art. The art is like a magnet calling me. Now I don't seem to have a way to express that part of myself. It's like being in a desert. I'm starting to connect to another, more genuine part of myself. The thing I'm most looking forward to is not being on a time schedule—having no responsibility to anyone but myself. I like to think I'm going to throw away all my watches.

—*Christine Golden, M.A., Middle School Principal*

 I have not given retirement much thought. Many of the choices and plans associated with retirement are already part of the goals and challenges of my everyday planning. I have been self-employed for most of my working life, so I don't have to make changes based on the criteria of an employer. Having increased freedom to do the things I want to do and a great financial plan are ongoing objectives.

I embrace my relationship to others with a recognition lacking in my youth. I look forward to increasing my interaction in the communities of the world. I am eager to unfold rewarding aspects of myself and sense that opening these places will be wholly rejuvenating—physically, emotionally and spiritually. Through my work, I grow in self-worth, self-identity and life skills. Personal achievement, overcoming life obstacles, expanding creativity through a lifestyle of "solutionism" holds within it unlimited potential for personal and professional expression. Why retire?

Now, a wake-up realization, the most important decision of my retirement planning: I will not take myself, or others, so seriously—a quantum leap for the bottom line of my development. Wisdom has prevailed. Expanding humor is now the first focus and primary requirement of my retirement initiative.

—*Jill Graham Adams, Owner and Director, Adams Healing Arts, Mystic, Connecticut*

Retirement can seem a far-off vista, one that might even be a bit foreboding. While we are young, becoming old doesn't seem to be real, and we tend to project our present health and vitality onto a future time.

 In a way it is easy for me to contemplate retirement. A vision of days steeped in leisure, travel and free creativity catapults me into fantasy. I imagine writing, painting, hiking through dense forests, traveling around the world, meditating at dawn and sunset, practicing yoga and qi gong and exercising regularly. I could learn to cook Thai food in Thailand, speak Spanish in Guatemala, surf in Australia, snowboard in New Zealand, or bicycle through Italy. I could volunteer with social and economic justice organizations, cultivate an organic vegetable and herb garden and make my own teas. I would spend more time with my family. All the things that I would do today if work did not exhaust so much of my time and energy.

Once begun, the fantasies of an active, joyful retirement come thick and fast. At the same time, I find it difficult to grasp a realistic vision of retirement, because I have no idea what the future holds, both for my personal life and for the world.

My mother retired in her mid-forties from a grueling job of low pay and low respect and now drives a van to deliver flowers in South Florida, where she brings a palpable joy to those she encounters. My father retired at age fifty-five from his career as a school social worker and after a few years of home health care and odd jobs, is writing his first novel. I do not think either one of them had this particular vision of retirement twenty or thirty years ago. But they both enjoy their current incarnations, and I hope that I may find the same satisfaction in my late middle age.

Is my imagination of the glories of retirement mere fantasy? I am thirty years from retirement. Thirty years! This seems an interminable length of time, practically double my life. Given the uncertainty of politics and social systems, I do not feel I can rely on the supports that appear automatic to today's retirees. Can I count on Social Security for income? What about Medicare? Will the onslaught of aging Boomers on our nationalized programs essentially eviscerate them? My small 401K seems unlikely to support me in old age, at least given its last few years' returns. I do not work for an employer who provides a pension. Just what can I count on thirty years from now? How will I support my leisure activities and world travel, let alone food, shelter and healthcare? I do not have answers to these questions.

Some would say we aren't able to count on anything, so why bother worrying about it? I normally do not think about my life in twenty or thirty years. It's just too far away. I focus on the present. The furthest into the future I have seriously considered is about two years. But I do live with intentions that I believe will continue through old age. I want to live my life in a socially conscious and responsible way. I want to continue to grow and learn and progress toward some sense of inner and outer peace. I want to stay healthy and fit. I want to invest and spend my money wisely with the least damage to humanity and the planet. I want to maintain connections with the people I love. I want to live a spiritual life and always be able to laugh, to have a sense of humor about myself and the world around me.

I suddenly realize that I have faith that I will be all right no matter what. Ultimately, whether or not Social Security and Medicare are available to me, *when* I retire is less important than *how* I live my life from day to day. But ask me thirty years from now. I might have a different story.

—*Kate Fallon, M.S.W., Dialysis Counselor*
*Portland, Oregon*

Kate's inner wisdom is illuminating. Who would not want to live with noble intentions throughout life's journey, reaping the blessings of socially conscious actions, growing, learning and progressing toward inner and outer peace and maintaining connections with loved ones. And all this founded upon a life of faith.

We can take encouragement from Kate's inspired yet pragmatic view of her future and trust that our spiritual strength will bolster us through the changes we will have to make.

## Layers

The clouds curl like fat cats in the deepening sky.
Shadows flirting across the sea's face
Lave dark wet kisses in the surf.
There, where sand and sea meet,
An egret skirts along the foam
Searching for succulent bits of food.
We are alone here,
This white bird and I.
Together we let the water wash our feet
And share a kinship of hunger.
We feed on beauty as we watch
A flight of brown pelicans dip down from the sky
in unison.
Wing tips touch on a wave's curl and they rise
Arcing up,
Then, catching a drift of wind,
They float like dark ships on an invisible sea.
The egret and I, finished with our feeding
Turn away from the water.
It looks at me with ancient eyes
As it spreads white wings to sail away.
My eyes join my heart to its flight
And we rise,
Flying together,
Out to Sea.

—Bonnie S. Bostrom

# Images of Power
## Leaving the CareerPerks Behind

If we look back in that rearview mirror to when we were young and beginning our careers, we see a time when women were struggling with newly won power. The women's movement was about claiming a foothold. It was about equality with men, freedom, and choice, and it was during this period that the notion of the everyday "superwoman" emerged. As women moved away from the homemaker role, they entered into a realm that for many required abandoning tasks of the heart—infants raised in child care settings, frozen TV dinners, hurried lives, husbands and lovers left behind.

The price was high for the rewards of a successful career. There was little or no time for self-reflection, or even the opportunity to ask, "Am I really happy?" However, once superwoman leaves the work arena, there is the very real probability that she will no longer consider herself super-anything.

Making money is part of the power equation—actually, a very large part. There is something deeply satisfying about exchanging creativity, time, and commitment for money. Money not only provides for basic life needs, it forms a link to power and status, producing what I call the new PMS — Power, Money, Status—the complete equation.

Our work personas are constantly made more real by the environment. Reverting to preset patterns becomes easier every day. The social context changes very little over time and this consistency is comfortable, familiar and reinforcing. Others see us through a filter shaped by this pattern, which in turn supports our behavior within the system. We content ourselves with a full desk, all our files in order, flow charts at the ready, day-planner at hand. We move within the building, hospital, center, airport, school, or courtroom with our boxes in tow, taking them from desk to desk.

When we leave or transfer away, the offices stay in the same preset hierarchy. Each new person who occupies an office assumes the inherent status of the position. We all move within the system, sometimes up or down, sometimes completely out, and that is when we have to take our boxes home.

We believe we are central to the system's process, but when we leave for good the system remains unchanged. It takes no note of the years of commitment and the sacrifices we made in the name of work. It remains impervious to the choices we made in order to keep the myth of our importance going, even at the expense of other relationships.

Power is tricky. We not only have conferred power, we also have personal power. Sometimes others are subject to our demands and we may fulfill our needs in such a way that we become more and more insular, more and more trapped in the work world.

 As the chair of an academic department, I had a number of faculty members who reported to me. Although we behaved as though there was absolute equality in our team, the reality was, I was still the "boss." If I wanted to go to lunch there was someone to go with. If I wanted intellectual stimulation I called a meeting and set the agenda. Funny, while this was going on I paid little attention to the fact that most of my social contacts were also my work contacts. When I left my position I found that I had to construct relationships in a whole new way. I had forgotten, if I ever knew, how to just be a friend, talk about things other than issues related to my work, truly engage in equitable connections.

—*Barbara Reider, Ph.D., former Chair, Education Department, College of Santa Fe*

We get addicted to the social image of ourselves in the workplace as well as to our titles. We form relationships because that is what women tend to do. However, professional relationships are subject to greater risk because they are work-dependent. The relationships are not often built on a foundation that carries over from the workplace to the outside; we leave alone. Our friends stay in their offices, still part of the system. We leave behind so much of ourselves—no wonder retirement can be such a troubling time.

The strength we felt while fulfilling the duties and opportunities of our positions nurtured us in a singularly specific way. Once we exit the workplace it is gone. That particular power, and the nurture we derived from it, is no longer available. When we find ourselves outside that familiar context, outside those patterns of interaction, we can be hit broadside with feelings of powerlessness.

 When you are working, you think you are in your power, and then when you leave work, you feel devastated. You have to move from working power to being power, to your true self, if you are lucky.

—*Felicite Woods, former Music Studio Manager Stamford, Connecticut*

Some women move into their true stride through work and the demands it makes on them, and it can take some doing to find the right niche. Finding our place in the world of work takes the courage to change and the determination to reach out for what we feel will be most fulfilling

If we make more money, we indulge in more extravagant

activities—take cruises, get a better car, help our kids and grandkids. But unless we have made a lot of money, saved well and survived stock market fluctuations, we will feel the pinch when we are no longer working.

 I was an X-ray tech starting at age seventeen, counting school, and took one year off when I had my daughter. After she was born I went on night call for seven years. Then I got a job with an orthopedic man and quit the hospital. I had planned to retire at sixty-five. After my husband took retirement, he encouraged me to quit early. I was still in my fifties.

We had started a craft shop out of our house. When we retired it grew into a fulltime pursuit. It was up in Old Forge, New York, in the Adirondacks. We ran the shop for ten years, selling crafts that we made and things that others made, especially the Amish people. One Amish family became such good friends that the husband still calls us from time to time from a neighbor's house. The Amish don't have phones.

Running the craft shop was very different from my work as an X-ray technician. When you are a tech, you are doing a service and people treat you with a certain kind of respect, probably respect for authority or something like that. It was different in the shop. It wasn't bad, but customers didn't treat me like a professional, if you know what I mean.

I missed the people I worked with in the hospital and I worked for thirty years in the same orthopedic office. We started with one doctor and then it grew to four doctors and they were all like family. I knew the patients and got to know their families. It wasn't the same in the shop. People would come and go and you couldn't really build a friendship with anyone.

We loved to snowmobile, but the time came when it was just too hard and too cold. There was snow several months of the year, and one day Joe came into the house and his hands were freezing and I looked at him and said, "What are we doing here? Let's go to Florida."

So I really retired when we got to Florida. It was such a relief not to have to get up and go to work or open the shop. At the same time, I didn't quite know what to do with myself. I'd just walk around the malls because I didn't have friends nearby and had no work to go to. I still get up early. It's a habit, and of course when you have four cats looking at you, you have no choice.

I don't know what I would have done without my friend who lives up the street. We went to school and did our training together and now we go places when we get a chance. We like to go shopping together and have lunch. We have known each other for such a long time.

I do like that I don't have to be on a schedule. And I never did rely on what I did for a living to provide my sense of self, so not working isn't that much of a change for me. I'm still the same person. I think the thing I miss most is making money. Things are tighter and we have to be more careful about how we spend money. Sometimes I worry about bills because the money isn't the same and I know I can't just go out and get another job. My knees don't give me a choice—they can't take it. Usually when I needed more money I just got a job, or a different job that paid better. Now work isn't an option. I can't work anymore.

*—Jean Farrell, former Radiological Technologist, North Jersey*
*Orthopedic Association, Pompton Plains, New Jersey*

Making money is glamorous. Payday makes everything seem possible and bright, full of potential. It gives us the right of way to options. We can afford to be, live, make decisions, buy things, and make plans. Letting go of money is no easy task and the phrase "having a fixed income" sounds like something has been neutered.

 When Friday of the second week came, I remembered I would not be getting paid. My employer always dispensed checks on Friday and even those with direct deposit got a summary of their earnings to date. I felt afraid and strangely anxious. I was not going to have my Friday fix—the paycheck. My retirement and savings were going to have to last me for a lifetime and I was certain it would not be enough. Even though my husband makes a very good living, I was mortally certain that there would not be enough money to survive.

For more than forty years, I always had a paycheck. I took time off to have my children, but only the company's standard maternity leave and always with the assurance that I would return to work and the paychecks would resume. I hadn't been conscious before of just how important that feeling of independence was. I was fearful of being dependent, and the paycheck was evidence of my independence.

I left my position as chief of education for an American Indian tribe before I reached the required age to apply for social security. Surprisingly, I was making an extraordinary six-figure salary. One doesn't usually associate wealth with educators or Indian tribes. This particular tribe has a highly successful casino and is quite generous with its employees, especially those they place in cabinet positions, and so I enjoyed a very comfortable and exciting lifestyle.

I know that part of the depression I felt upon retiring had to do with leaving the money. Before going to work for the tribe I had earned a far more "normal" income in my position as executive director of a leadership-development project at a university in the southwest. My salary at the tribe was far more than I had ever made, or had even dreamed of making, as an educator. It was a deeply affirming experience. It was delightful. Making lots of money became a cornerstone of security, an internal home base where I could rest easy, not worry about having enough and occasionally feel giddy with exhilaration. I loved thinking such thoughts as, "I make a better salary than most men," and I particularly relished thinking, "If they could only see me now," of people who had used power positions to take advantage of me in the past.

I was raised in abject poverty and made small gains through hard work. This was a beautiful setup for the money to go to my head. I felt excited about my work in the beginning, true, but the validation of having someone pay me that much to manage, think and lead—that was addictive. When I finally realized that I was truly addicted to the money and that my day-to-day experience was unfulfilling, it became apparent that I would have to leave. I would have to leave the job and I would have to leave that lovely money. Understand, I had not become an unfeeling, wretched being. I was a good, kind human being. The simple fact was, the work became un-interesting and intellectually unchallenging. I was unhappy.

I stayed in the "golden handcuffs" for several months, trying to come to grips with what was happening to me. I couldn't believe that I was planning to quit my job, and that I was going to walk away from the security, the lifestyle, and the fantastic ego trip just because I was bored. But I did it.

When I turned sixty-two I talked with a financial advisor who recommended that I apply for Social Security early. He explained that if I decided to wait until I became sixty-five to get the higher amount I wouldn't break even until after I turned eighty. I elected to follow his advice and called the Social Security office. I was absolutely amazed at how simple the process was. I called them and gave them the information over the phone, they sent the application to me, I returned it with a copy of my birth certificate and that was it. They returned my birth certificate and told me I should receive my first check in about three weeks.

Filling out the forms was simple, but applying for benefits was not. It brought with it the sobering reminder that I was no longer making a lot of money. In fact, I wasn't *making* any money. I was retiring and would be on a fixed income. Talk about boring. My prior thoughts about nobility of purpose and the ignobility of working in a lackluster job because it pays well seemed sophomoric and self-indulgent.

—*Bonnie S. Bostrom*

Thus we find ourselves giving up power, money, and status in exchange for the poor replacements of depression, fear of dependency and feelings of inadequacy. We are shocked at the depth and tenacity of the anger we feel when we sense we have lost ourselves. Or we begin to suspect that what we lost was an illusion.

Work defines us to a great degree. Our sense of self becomes saturated with the power we wield, and while it may be positional, it still forms a large part of our self-identity. We are complicit in constructing this work self, and because we create it in part from aspects of our true self, it is hard to separate the two. Like Siamese twins, personal and positional power have shared boundaries. Without the structure and holding patterns constantly in place in the work environment, the social construct of the self begins to unravel.

 I worked for fifteen years as an editor/administrator for a nonprofit organization, doing everything from policy work with the board of directors to training volunteers and working as a personal assistant.

After a huge upheaval in the organization I found myself out of a job. I panicked. My income was gone, my professional development interrupted and I had lost face. I felt valueless, as though I'd been demoted to a non-person. I knew I was competent, so I could deal with a portion of the panic logically, but much of it was irrational.

After the initial shock and panic, I became angry and resentful that there had been this huge disturbance. Some anger was directed toward the politics of my situation and some toward its basic unfairness.

Next came the feeling that I didn't know what to do combined with incredulity at *acknowledging* that I didn't know what to do. It was interesting because I was very invested in being that person— the title, the position. All of that was far more important than I realized. I was stupefied.

I was not well networked because of the nature of the organization. I found myself in a small town, without a job and without a network. I had this sense that my skills were so specialized that they would not transfer to another situation.

All those discursive thoughts about what was going on were attempts to avoid looking at the chasm. I went into free-fall.

The free-fall syndrome started up pretty quickly, but it took me awhile to recognize that I lacked the sense of identity that came from my work, and it was a bit shocking to see how all encompassing it was. Every area of my life was affected. In other words, I had evolved to where my life was structured completely around my work. I had no idea what I wanted to do when I found myself without that structure.

I was reminded of an incident some years earlier when I was getting acupuncture treatments and the technician suggested that I take time for some self-nurturing. She asked me what I liked to do, and I just went blank. I was so enmeshed in my work and taking care of my family that I couldn't even think that way. After a few minutes, with a little coaxing, she got me to recollect things I had done when I was single. I remembered yoga and dance. It wasn't that I had a faulty memory, I was so heavily ingrained with one way of thinking that I had to make a real effort to jump the tracks and think in a different way.

So this free-fall was basically very much like that, but larger, because I discovered that not only was I without the familiar reference points of my identity, I didn't know how to think of myself. In other words, the loss of identity went far deeper than I ever imagined it could. Wow! It was like being on the downhill run of the roller coaster, or jumping out of the plane for a little skydiving.

My training in meditation tells me that these free-fall moments happen all the time, but we quickly fill up the space with lots of thoughts that confirm who we are. However, sometimes the gap is so huge you can't fill it in quickly enough. I saw this, and even though there was a degree of panic, I also felt that it was an important opportunity not to repeat the habitual patterns of the past, but to hang out in that space—fall through it, hold still, and simply be aware. So I made a concerted effort to let things come to me, rather than to embark on a reconstruction project.

During this "falling" period, I saw that I had to work very carefully on self-confidence and always go to the root of myself, apart from a job identity. Again, I didn't think I had so much invested in that job, but every day I saw where I had built up all kinds of little "stories" about myself, to myself, that had a lot to do with self-confidence and self-esteem.

> —*Donna Holm, former Deputy Director, Vajradhatu Buddhist Church; currently Senior Editor, Vajradhatu Publications, Halifax, Nova Scotia*

Sometimes we are able to ferret out our emotions, name them, confront them, and stand them down. We aren't always pleased by what we see staring back at us from the mirror. It takes courage to look at ourselves and to own what we see.

 What I did not expect was the anger. Total fury directed everywhere and nowhere. It seemed that my office, my position and my power were taken over by vultures. The vultures had been in wait and I had considered them my friends. I felt that I had died. All those years and all those times that I had to make the decision, carry the load, frequently take the heat— you would think "they" would be more grateful. You would think they would call me sometimes just to ask my advice or at least where I had put a file! I am told "they" did not want to bother me. I had decided to leave and therefore I should be granted the respect of distance. I felt negated. How could all of this go on without me? How could other people move into my office, my position, my power, without even acknowledging that I, not they, was really needed to make things work?

If you asked them they would probably be astounded that I felt this way. I offered so many times to help if I could, with any and all transitions, but I was met with anger and resistance. I did leave *them*, didn't I?

It is really a strange experience, this retirement. It is more about loss than I first realized. I am still doing many things very much tied to my profession. I am creating new paths with old and new professional friends. I know logically I have no reason to be angry. I had expected depression, but not this. It is almost as though I am invisible to the mirror I used for so long. I know that this is an opportunity to find the mirror within myself—finally and forever.

—*Barbara Reider*

Every woman must come to terms with the things she leaves behind. We watch children who finally let go of the blanket or the dilapidated doll that couldn't be out of sight for a second and we feel a tinge of sadness. It's as though we want to say, "Wait, you can't throw your baby away. Don't you want your blankey anymore?" They may be ready, but something in us wants them to hold on just a little bit longer. Soon we will have to start letting go of *them*. They will move out, go to college, find life partners, and we will be left behind. Like the blanket or the doll.

We say goodbye to our grandparents and, after a time, our parents leave us. We are aging orphans in the world. So we cling to the blanket of work in a world that is beginning to fill with losses. Then, when we let go of work, the sadness feels all too familiar. We are the little girl letting go of her doll, we are the mother watching as her daughter tosses the blanket aside and goes outside to play. We are bravely letting go of the crazy quilt of work and all the illusions that it brought. We are emptying out the desk.

# 4

# When the Mirror Breaks
## The Painful Reality of Forced Retirement

We don't always hit some magic age and decide to quit our jobs. Sometimes the decision is made for us, or forced upon us by circumstance. Regardless of the specific catalyst, retirement brings with it attendant emotions—some good, some scary, and some difficult to define.

 I'm not sure I'm in the "retired" category. I am fifty-seven and have worked most of my adult life, except when my children were young. I went to work fulltime in 1981. I have an associate's degree in applied science and am also a licensed insurance agent in Texas. My work background ranges from business owner to office administrator with everything clerical in between.

I didn't exactly retire. I simply quit my job because my employer intended to cut my hours and pay. I didn't want to work part-time so I gave notice. I haven't decided for sure whether to retire permanently or not.

Right now I'm feeling very uncertain about everything. I'm not sure what I want to do. I've decided to take control of my own destiny instead of letting other people decide how I fit into the work force. That decision is a little scary. It really rubbed me the wrong way to think that another person had enough control over me to decide the number of hours a week I worked.

Did I do the right thing? Do I really want to retire? Can I find something else if I want to? I don't know. The uncertainty is what's bugging me. I just have to accept that nothing in life is certain and then take the time to decide what's right for me at this point in my life.

—*Dovie St. Peters, Licensed Insurance Agent, State of Texas*

When we are forced out, fired, or have no control over decisions that precipitate our leaving, the depression seems to be compounded. A sense of autonomy is so crucial to our wellbeing that when we feel powerless, we become deeply angry. Without avenues for alleviating the anger, the depression can become acute, perhaps even make us ill. Though technically unrelated to work, the resulting illness exacerbates an already difficult situation.

I am an artist and graphic designer. I stopped working in the corporate world when I became pregnant. I could not continue with the kind of work I was doing. The deadlines were stressful and I had to do large, physically-demanding airbrush projects. The pressure was pervasive. I also wanted to be with my child, an unexpected miracle.

After having worked constantly for twenty years I found myself, at forty-two, at home with a new baby, in a new town, with an unraveling marriage. There was no support system. My own family were all still in Brazil and I felt scared, lonely, unappreciated and powerless in my situation. I believe I was going through post-partum depression. I went to a therapist after I was already separated from my husband and the therapist didn't even pick up on the fact that I was depressed. I was very adept at displaying a happy face.

So many things were happening at once, I can't sort out what was really going on. Once I picked up a survey on stress and found that I had every negative factor on the scale. Funny, I feel more powerful now, even though I have no money, no job and no visible security.

When my daughter was just three, I found that I had cancer—

non-Hodgkins lymphoma. I learned that this particular cancer comes in twelve subdivisions ranging from types that kill you fast to those that kill you slowly. Having a slow type gives me time to reflect and study myself. Hopefully I will see my daughter grow up and become a woman.

I am lucky, because looking death in the face inspires me to want to become the best person I can be. I have nothing material to give my daughter, so I want to give her the best possible me.

This desire has propelled me to do a lot of internal work, some of it, maybe most of it, unpleasant. It has allowed me to see that what is important is not the job you have, but the legacy you leave behind. People are not going to remember what I did for a living; they will remember who I was. My true identity—the identity I want to share with my community—is a goal worth working for. I want to find the root of myself and then share the branches.

It has not been an easy journey for me, though my study of Buddhist and Taoist thinking has made it easier. I am feeling much more compassionate toward myself, which I think translates into more compassion for others. I'm more productive and creative than ever before.

Fortunately my ex-husband has helped me with our daughter. Working freelance provides needed income, and I keep working on myself. I will always have my art. I just won't ever have another job.

—*Silvia Almeida, Freelance Artist and Graphic Designer*
*Norwich, Connecticut*

Most of us don't realize how deeply our entire being is embedded with work. Work permeates everything, defining and nourishing us in ways we don't see until we step away from it. Work becomes the "Thou" in the "I-Thou" relationship, a strange, singularly important significant other. When we step away from this relationship to respond to the needs of others (a child at home, a husband who is retiring), we sacrifice our work life. These sacrifices are thrust upon us and the resulting departures are unplanned.

 One of the saddest things I've learned about retirement I discovered when my husband retired. We had always assumed that when he retired I would be able to do anything I chose. But I was already doing what I wanted, exactly what I wanted. I had built a very successful interior design business and was happily engaged in helping other women realize their visions of the perfect home. The business was successful because I used my creativity to assist women who sometimes had only vague ideas about what would bring them joy.

I know that material possessions in themselves don't bring happiness, but they can provide beauty and a sense of identity. When a woman chooses the perfect fabric, or carries in some treasure from the attic, she is often choosing a lovely centerpiece for not only her home but her heart.

Many of my suburban clients were newly transferred and had lost their best friend, their hairdresser and their identity. So I not only helped them get used to their new homes, I helped them accept their new lives.

When my husband retired, I unexpectedly became one of those women. When we left his job, we left mine too. Only I didn't choose to leave. I did it to be with my husband and to make him happy. I sacrificed, and it was painful.

We lived together on a boat for two years. I enjoyed the time and cherish the experience. I thought, "If I have to leave everything that seems important, at least I am moving toward a great adventure."

Eventually we gave up our nomadic lifestyle, moved to Florida and started unpacking boxes. It's strange how we collect meaningful mementos, but stranger still that all these things don't fill the emptiness when part of us is gone. I'm sure I will learn something from this time of introspection and recreation. Maybe my experiences with all those other displaced women will help me to put my own house in order and become happy in my new life.

—*Carla Christianson, former Interior Designer*
*Palm Coast, Florida*

Some decisions are made for us. We don't leave a job because our husband is retiring or, because we want to do something different. Our work is taken from us because of a merger or economic downturn. Sometimes we have no voice in the decision, no choice in the matter at all.

I have been in transition all of my life. I started making decisions and playing my role in the world at eighteen. I realize now how many times I set goals and acted on what I thought I should be doing, rather than what I truly wanted. I *should* get married, *should* be a good Catholic, *should* be responsible, *should* do the right thing, *should* think of others. I always made a plan and brought it to closure.

When I was a young woman my beloved fiancé was killed in a car accident, and work became my salvation. Work helped me to deal with the grief, grief that I feel to this day. Work became everything and it remained the stabilizing force in my life. Work was always there and it got me through a painful marriage and divorce and numerous other disappointments.

Getting things done was easy for me. I am adaptable and skilled at accessing new knowledge and applying it. I used work as therapy, so it is no surprise that I achieved in my chosen field of healthcare administration. It was a surprise when I was downsized. When work, the panacea, is suddenly gone, where do you turn for help?

At first I hardly knew how to react and wasn't sure if I was upset or relieved.

I went where I always go. I went to church. It may sound unusual, but as a young girl and throughout my life I have always gone into churches when there was no one else around. I go up and lie in front of the altar on the dais. So that's what I did. I went into the church near my apartment and stayed there on the dais for two hours. During the final days of my tenure at the hospital I spent time there daily, staring at the ceiling, praying, meditating and trying to sort out my feelings.

Looking back, I would have expected the loss to hurt more, but I am changing inside. I realize that I am young enough, and perhaps strong enough, to finally set a goal that I truly want. I am taking some time and exploring the best way to enact my new plan. I want to live for me, for my true desires, and in that living I hope that I will be able to help others. But this time the helping others has to be secondary. I am going to live for myself while I still have the chance.

—*Georgeann Raco, former Hospital Health Administrator*
*Miami, Florida*

## Accepting who we are and our changing circumstances can mitigate any sense of powerlessness, sadness, and anger

we have at our situations. As we progress through this transition we look around us. And sometimes we look directly into the mirror.

# Disrobing Before the Mirror
## Aging in a Society Dedicated to Youth

Naked, we feel ultra vulnerable. As we grow older, the mirror is not the friend it was when we were young and fit. We may still spend a lot of time before the mirror, but we gaze with a far more critical eye.

The end of employment doesn't happen when we are seventeen or twenty-seven, with clear eyes, smooth skin, good legs and endless vitality. It happens when menopause is slapping us sideways, when plastic surgery doesn't seem like such an unnatural act, and when we are getting both wider and shorter. Our children, if there are any, have moved away and started their own families. The nest is empty and we have been leaving it daily, flying off to work. Now we are going to be in the nest all day long, with mirrors everywhere. We look everywhere for metaphors to explain what is happening to us. Sometimes, we are surprised at how the universe responds.

There is a story about a turtle that was mugged by a snail. When the turtle was asked for details about the event it responded, "I don't know. It just all happened so fast." Like the turtle, we feel as though we are being mugged in slow motion. The culprit is time—time and gravity.

Our culture tends to equate femininity with fecundity and fertility. America pretends that only young people have sex, are sensual and attractive, and we are still so influenced by Puritanism, harking back to Victorianism, we pretend that people past childbearing age don't have sex. After all, sex at a later age would have to be for pleasure. Our wholesale cultural ban on indulging in sex for pleasure is threatened by gays, lesbians and old people. We can accept sexuality and sexual behavior in young people because they can, and must, procreate if we intend to remain a species on the planet. Blaming their hormones puts boundaries around sexual behavior, circumscribing youth and married couples fairly comfortably. Anything outside those boundaries is rejected, tolerated at best.

How many women are avoiding their doctor's recommendation to get off hormone-replacement therapy and are taking hormones long after they are necessary to relieve symptoms of menopause, just because they want to hold on to youth, and to sexual desire? How many of us believed that estrogen was the answer—still believe it? Now research tells us that hormone replacement therapy is deleterious and doesn't really provide all those protections. Yet we bought those pills and swallowed them month after month, believing that they would delay the steady oncoming march of age.

Research reports insist that people in their mature years enjoy a robust sex life. No one expected that old people would be having sex, and, furthermore, having sex for fun. There is a story about a very old man who married a young woman and soon it was obvious that the woman was pregnant. All the people in their small town were whispering and sharing knowing glances, convinced that the old man was being played for the fool until one discerning fellow said, "Well, consider this: the old man *thinks* that's his baby."

So, old people have sex and old men can father children. Our culture doesn't really approve, but our cultural demographic is changing so there are more young and more old than before. A significant difference separates them: greater poverty among the young. It will be interesting to see how our culture changes when one side of the scale is weighted by age and money and the other by youth and poverty.

In this flourishing youth culture, we aging boomers are running after a last chance to appear young by spending our money to buy it. Surgery, spas, exercise, massage, relaxation tapes—you name it, we buy it. And we are still growing old. Maybe our culture will change, will begin to appreciate us, even emulate us. Maybe as we grow older we will become more accepting of who we are and how we look.

*And...*
*Let us open our legs*
*And cherish each other*
*And welcome deep thrusts*
*And lift wise breasts up*
*To be drunk from,*
*And taste tongues*
*And sleep tangled into each other's arms*
*And celebrate we have no children now to disturb*
*Our sleep,*
*And we cannot get pregnant*
*And our limbs move still*
*And we pee into the earth unrestrained*
*And no one comments when our hair falls out.*
*And our lips, our lips smile and scowl and taste*
*Everything*
*And our bodies are heart shaped and eager for life*
*One more day.*

—Katherine Moore

Clothing designers cater to professional women and the youth culture. The rest of us are expected to be delighted with a cover-the-body-from-head-to-toe sack. Sure, we can buy outfits adorned with beaded butterflies and fancy knit sweaters made of pretend gold and silver thread. That's not the point. Very few designers cater to older women because they assume we will be home where no one will see us and therefore don't care how we look. Furthermore, many designers don't sell clothes in sizes over twelve because they think larger women make the clothes look bad.

So we get the idea that we aren't attractive, because we don't look young anymore. We go for the clothes that hide our natural evolution, dye our beautiful silver hair and worry about losing our husbands, lovers and partners. We dread the mirror, but we can't hide—not from ourselves and not from a society that values attributes we no longer have in the way we did when we were girls, young women, or even middle aged. If we look carefully, though, we may see something we weren't expecting.

*Poem for Everywoman*
*What am I concerned with?*
*Look in the mirror – gray hairs, facial lines, sagging breasts,*
*Pot belly, wrinkly papyrus skin,*
*Spreading hair, flabby thighs,*
*Varicose veins, purple feet.*
*The powder of my deodorant makes*
*A circle above my breast, where my breast used to start.*
*Now it's two inches lower.*
*The curves are still pleasing, though.*
*The softness is softer,*
*The eyes more forgiving,*
*The mouth more tender.*
*The smile is brighter.*
—Carol McDermott

Remember when we used to play dress-up? As little girls we could be outrageously daring, deliciously beautiful. Old tea towels were magically made into trains that dragged behind us as we danced toward womanhood. We bedecked ourselves with bracelets made from Mason jar rings and never considered playing someone old. Old people were mean and did terrible things to children. We wanted the part of the princess. We were practicing for the rituals of womanhood, following a preset pattern that had us all living happily ever after. Our fantasies ended with a kiss, or a coronation, or a grand party. They never ended with us becoming old.

 The whole notion of applying for Social Security brought up feelings about aging, about being old and unattractive. That was another illusion that earning money had provided: I felt more attractive with a paycheck. The whole self-esteem-power-beauty package was a real driver for me. I had never been long on physical beauty, but prided myself in intellectual accomplishments and creative products like poetry and music. When I was making money I felt fantastic, beautiful and glamorous. I looked just the same, mind you—it was how I felt about myself that was different. It wasn't until I left work that the illusion collapsed and my mirror reflected a more realistic image. I could see a tall, matronly woman with wrinkling skin, graying hair, hazel eyes and a kindly smile. Not bad, but certainly not beautiful. I like myself without the illusion, but I must admit there were aspects of the fantasy that were appealing. Life offers many traps. It's hard to avoid unwittingly falling into them.

When my bank statement reflected the arrival of the first Social Security check, I was thrilled. It was amazing. My Friday paycheck was miraculously back and my sense of feeling very dependent upon my husband changed when I realized that this was *my* money. I had earned this money and I was once again getting paid. This time I was paying myself and I loved it. Applying for, and getting, my Social Security is one of the best things I've ever done. I feel independent, solvent, and it provides me with an unprecedented opportunity. I can write now. It seems that all my life I have been grabbing little pieces of time for myself so that I could write a poem, or an article, or something I needed to say in more formal language. Writing was something I deserved to do only if all my other commitments were met. It wasn't something I could stay home from work to do, or do before the groceries were bought, dinner made, e-mails sent, or thank-you cards mailed. You name it—it came before writing. Writing was frivolous. Teachers touted typing, but you were expected to become a secretary not a poet. Poets don't make money. And it's true, of course, but what I've found is that money doesn't make poetry either.

I'm not sure where my new life is going, but I know that I am going with it, not against it. When I was working in a job that left me unfulfilled, that left my intellect unchallenged and my potential masked in the obscurity of power and money, I was a counterforce. The mirror of work didn't exactly reflect an identity for me. Instead, I projected onto that mirror all the sociological constructs that I had accepted as valid representations of who I was. Someone else has my old job while I have my old self. I am emerging from the limiting world of work into the freedom of creative being. And I am writing poetry!

### Women and Glass

*I have a fascination with glass.*
*I recall clearly that splendid moment*
*Descending the staircase*
*All shining.*
*A prelude to the magic*
*When the slipper glistened upon my foot.*

*And the sisterhood on an island*
*Where my beauty and daring*
*Won for me the golden lasso,*
*Belt and crown*
*And where I flew beyond our ancient secrets*
*In my airplane made of glass.*
*I can hear the horse's hooves*
*Chiming as they strike their way*
*Up glass mountain.*
*I can see the winning knight*
*Approach the palace to find my heart.*
*All men are heroes when seen*
*Through glass from a distant tower.*

*Now my beauty breaks*
*Inside the mirror on the wall and age,*
*That wicked stepmother,*
*Bids me stay awhile and play*
*With bits and pieces of broken glass.*

—Bonnie S. Bostrom

Part of going to work was getting ready for work. Getting the wardrobe organized for the seasons, finding clothes that traveled well and dressing for success. It was an adult form of dress-up.

We don't always think of the simple traditions as rituals. They seem like normal everyday activities. Some of those rituals sustain us in subtle ways. When they are no longer a priority or necessity we miss them.

I had not planned to quit. I was fifty-two at the time, working as an administrative assistant for a marine sciences institute. The state came out with a program that offered early retirement, paid-up life insurance and free medical coverage for life for my husband and me. I decided I should take it, since I didn't know if the package would be offered again and, besides that, I wasn't happy with the job.

I remember it was the first of March and my husband Ben went off to work. I woke up and thought, "What am I going to do with the rest of my life?"

I went crazy with boredom. My friends were all still working. I had no hobbies. I felt like I was floating on an iceberg. I watched stupid talk shows, knit some and read. After two weeks I'd had it. I went to work for Kelly Temporary Services and continued on and off for three years.

I retired the second time because I burned out, lost interest in the job. Now my husband is retired and I love being home, though I miss the social contacts of work.

My husband and I think of something special to do every day. We go to the library for two hours and read about stocks we might like to buy, or we make a big deal of a trip to WalMart. We've had time to travel to Alaska.

I've taken up golfing and still knit. I hate talking on the phone, so I don't call my kids and I don't mind being alone. I get on the computer and check stocks, or look at travel magazines for bargains.

When I first quit I would wake up at six-fifteen and then happily go back to sleep. That was the best thing about retirement. The worst part is lack of coworker interaction and, of course, the loss of money.

I feel badly because I have really beautiful jewelry and no place to wear it. Sometimes I wear my Gucci watch with blue jeans. I gave all my good work clothes to Goodwill. Actually, it's a dull life and I think I'll go back to work next year.

—*Eleanor Minic, former Administrative Assistant, Marine Sciences Institute, Connecticut*

Some women are able to incorporate dress-up in their new rituals, making it a part of everyday activities. Since we discovered how to decorate our faces with clay and iron-rich mud, we have been attempting to make ourselves look beautiful, or different. When we don't groom ourselves it's usually a dead giveaway that we are depressed or not doing well. Women love to prepare for special occasions. We lay our garments on the bed, choose earrings with tremendous care, decide on shoes and check ourselves carefully to ensure we are dressed exactly right for the event.

 My lack of energy and inability to do a lot of the physical things I once did makes finding things to do more difficult. Going to breakfast every day may sound trivial, but it gets me out. I look forward to it and plan what I am going to wear. I dress well, which makes me feel my best. I think it makes others feel good to see someone all fixed up and looking nice, so I take a lot of care to dress well. Then, when I go into a restaurant and people say, "Hello, Rita," it's just great.
—*Rita Herbert, former Division Manager, Thomas Flynn Orchids, Division of Vaughan Seed Company*
*Bound Brook, New Jersey*

Some part of the female psyche is inextricably drawn to the role of actor. As children we stage great theatricals, act out stories and play at real life. Part of that play continues into the world of work. We dress for work, for play, for bed—all different actions, different roles.

 One of my biggest retirement issues was what to do with all my clothes. The shoes, pants, skirts, even the socks that touched the workplace were sacrosanct. These clothes could never be worn on a non-workday, even though a duplicate pair of pants in another color was acceptable for Saturday errands. Work was a special place and I was a different person there. My clothes were the costume, the workplace my stage. How terrible to believe my acting days are over.
—*Barbara Reider*

Sometimes we can catch a glimpse of the role we are playing and identify the meta-narrative behind our actions. Familiar feelings lie behind what seem to be first time experiences. We are, at once, actor and witness to what we are doing in the world. We sense the script, we know we are doing something that has been done a thousand times before, and told in a thousand stories.

 When a friend came to visit shortly after I left work, I took her upstairs to my closet and asked her if she wanted some of my clothes. We have similar coloring and height, so I knew the clothes would fit and would look becoming on her. As I took each garment from the hook and handed it to her, she would exclaim delight in the color, fabric or style. Soon she was trying them on and dashing downstairs to let her husband view yet another wonderful new outfit. As we continued, I became her handmaiden, her dresser, preparing her for another trip down the stairs to "show off." In a black dress with bright red trim she was Little Red Riding Hood. She donned a brown-and-tan set and became Jo from *Little Women*. Velvet summoned the fairy queen and a gray wool dress with matching cape beckoned Cathy in from the moors.

I was the fairy godmother, she was Cinderella, and we were playing dress-up—little girls once again. How deeply embedded are the stories of our childhood, those meta-narratives. So much so that we don't notice the invisible frames through which we view our lives until retirement gives us the time to see through those frames again. I am reminded of two favorite lines of poetry from Pindar, "Will they come again, ever again, the long, long dances."

—*Bonnie S. Bostrom*

## Meeting Again

I saw her face reflected.
The wide shining windows at The Top of the Mark
sent it to me against the backdrop of San Francisco lights.
I knew she was remembering her dervish days,
Twirling and spinning round a windmill pipe.
She had seen Saturn make his seven year trek
full three times and was celebrating
having negotiated the turning.
Once she was wearing a hat that stopped my heart
when I spied her in a storefront glass
as I strolled along Grant Avenue.
It was improbably filled with flowers on a brim so wide
it caught ocean mist and twilight
and I'm sure I caught the scent of sea foam
as she paso dobled past.
I saw her brown-skinned and freckled boarding a late flight
from Oaxaca to the states.
Her smile said a thousand secrets had been spoken in the hot sand
and the hot air on Play Del Ropa.
She loved Jazz in the City;
Everyone from San Francisco calls it the City.
She has smiled that love to me from the bottom of a glass
of Scotch "neat"
while she listened to Cannonball Adderley
and told outrageous tales to attractive strangers.
Contemporary Dancers Workshop on Polk Street
was a harbor for her heart
and anchored her gypsy feet to dazzling patterns
while all the mirrors in the room silently applauded.
I lost touch with her, as we do, and then,
just the other day, while driving,
I heard a cut by Cannonball Adderley
and there she was,
the woman I used to be.

—Bonnie S. Bostrom

# 6

## *Dragons in the Mirror*
### *Dealing with Post-Retirement Depression*

Early mapmakers didn't know what lay beyond charted territory, so they warned of dragons. The first few days and weeks of retirement can be filled with dragons. Some women are surprised, even a bit scared, when they run head-on into deeply engrained old habits. When my writing partner, Barbara, realized that she was depressed, she took the opportunity to explore the meaning of her emotional dive.

 I constructed my relationships around work, my time around work and, maybe most important, the "I" that I thought was really me around work. Work was a safe place, a protected place, a place where the parts of me I did not want to listen to could be kept at bay.

The depression was related to my unwillingness to grieve for the life I had prior to retiring. Grieving requires giving up the illusion of safety. The process of retiring goes beyond leaving a job, or changes in income, lifestyle and time management. Retiring required changes beyond those connected to my work life.

When I left one of my earliest professional positions to have a child, I needed to take my nameplate with me. The plate bore my name, of course, but more importantly it spelled out my position. Years later when I left my position as chair of an education department at a small liberal arts college, I gave my name plate to my assistant. I explained that I no longer needed it to tell me who I was. Certainly a noble gesture and one that suggested I was aware of the identity issue that had surrounded my adult life: if I am not my nameplate, then who am I?

So what is this depression affecting me? I am now sixty, not twenty-eight as I was when I left my first really exciting professional position. I am facing the end, not the beginning of my career (and, in many ways, my life). Who am I when there is no external identifying shape to give me identity? My depression may actually come from trying to find the answer to that question.

One would expect this to be an exciting time of self-discovery, a time when my "real self," whatever that is, could find expression. Such optimism is commendable, but not natural to me. For me, this is just hard work with an intellectual overlay of opportunity, the possibility of personal evolution and, of course, a chance to do whatever I have always wanted.

But the major problem with the argument that now I can do what I always wanted is, I have *been* doing what I always wanted. I have problems with people who view their work as something that enables them to play. Work to me *was* play—my creative space, my source of personal power and self-worth.

My depression results from losing this former playground, and from the fear that I won't find another quite so sweet. Is there any other playground for the kind of internal sense of power, accomplishment and creativity that I found in my job? That's the question.

Why did I retire in the first place? I was not asked to retire by my employer. I did not have any great plans for what else to do with my life. Fortunately, I still have both good health and a very capable mind.

I suppose I knew deep down the path I was on, even though the voice giving the guidance was very difficult to hear. I knew that if I didn't leave, I would begin to do less well the things I had always done superbly. The voice inside, although quiet, insisted that it was time to move on, not professionally, but personally. What did I lose during all those years when I used my professional mask to avoid knowing myself in other realms and at different levels? This is the task retirement has given me.

At first I was incredibly frightened by the space left when the job was no longer there to provide content for my life. I was suddenly without an umbilical cord to my identity. So without taking time to really think, I quickly partnered with a colleague from the college and filled that fearful space with new work.

However, my colleague is not always available, so I am compelled to occupy my time and, more importantly, my mind with more than work. I am forced to find other ways to ground myself. The depression stems in part from being unable to sustain my immersion in work. I am re-patterning my brain, creating new shapes of the self against a completely foreign backdrop.

I wonder what the space created by my retirement would have looked like if I had not rushed to fill it with just anything. Could I have surrendered to that space? Could I have seen it with new eyes? Or would I have been so overwhelmed by the anxiety of emptiness, the disorientation about who I am, as to stop functioning altogether? Maybe, for me, creating only a partial space was necessary. Maybe there is no one best way to do this retirement stuff.

Retirement provides an opportunity to connect and reconnect to the parts of yourself that got lost during the years when work prevailed. An opportunity to connect to the parts you never knew, but have always been there and worth knowing.

—*Barbara Reider*

Depression is not news to women. The lack of forewarning is. There are no billboards saying, "Beware, rocky times ahead," "Depression is common when you retire," or "Watch for sudden feelings of despair followed by listlessness and boredom when you leave the workplace." We understand post-partum depression to some extent, and pre-menstrual stress, and we know about the empty nest syndrome, but this is different (though some of the feelings are familiar). This is the empty desk syndrome.

I found myself haunted by habitual urgings, and my mind kept moving toward the old familiar patterns of my former life. I also found myself falling into depression and was shocked at how quickly and deeply it developed. Climbing out of the depression is the first step toward survival, but it isn't easy. First, you have to get out of bed.

One of the things I discovered almost immediately was that my whole system was geared around work and work schedules. My last day was a Friday, so the first weekend seemed like a normal Saturday and Sunday. On Sunday evening I felt an urge to pick out the clothes I was going to wear to work the next day. My mind flitted from wondering if I had plenty of gas in the car to trying to remember where I had put my day-planner.

The next day I discovered that my internal gears did not readily adjust to my new freedom. I wanted to call the extension numbers of people I had seen daily for years. It seemed like I should phone people at the office to let them know I wouldn't be coming in. I felt like having a meeting, or making a priorities list. Later in the afternoon, I felt absolutely deflated. By Wednesday of the first week, I had cleaned out all my closets, played guitar until my fingers rebelled and caught up on personal correspondence.

By the following Friday I was in deep depression. Before leaving my job I had thought how wonderful it would be to have all the time I wanted to do all those things I had never really had time to do. I found that you don't play the guitar for eight hours a day, and clean closets just don't provide the satisfaction that problem solving does. In fact, all those things I never had time for didn't require much time. One day I got up, ate breakfast, walked two miles on the treadmill, did the laundry, baked brownies, tidied the entire house, gave up caffeine, caught up with all my e-mail, gave myself a facial and it was only 11:30 in the morning. I knew I had to assess my situation.

—*Bonnie S. Bostrom*

Hyperbole aside, realizing that you might be depressed is difficult, especially if you imagined your new life would afford opportunities for all that self-expression and relaxation you had set aside for later.

The images we have about retirement are born of societal messages that start in kindergarten, where play and work are separate endeavors. Like eating dessert after enduring the misery of a detested vegetable, play is a reward that follows hard work. The idea that one's work could also be play is a particularly difficult concept for many, adding to already complex feelings about retirement.

 I never thought of the work I did as work in the traditional sense. I had fun! I loved the creativity of my job. Since I was a child, I've thought of creative activities as play. I did not even like to use the phrase, "going to work." It sounded like I was supposed to be very serious all the time—very adult. People kept asking me how I would "play" after I retired. I had no answer, since I was already playing. This was the recreation I knew. Sure, I loved to hike, camp, and work out at the gym, but I did not think these activities were meant to replace my work play. If I was already playing, then what did retirement have to offer me?

—*Barbara Reider*

Play is an important aspect of life. When we think of retirement, we often envision it as the opportunity for more play. For some, it is picking up on hobbies, for others taking up a new sport or trying a hand at painting or pottery. If you were already engaged in gratifying leisure, the idea seems redundant. If retirement is, in part, an opportunity to do the things you did not have time to do before—to play at new games so to speak—what happens to those of us who were already doing what we wanted to do, who did not wait to play?

The newly created space afforded by retirement does not necessarily bring the sense of joy we anticipated. We have finally arrived at the destination toward which we've been headed: career, success, retirement and leisure. It's hard to admit that we're not happy. After all, we've worked hard for this and it should feel great. But it doesn't. It's a shock to find that instead of being happy we are sad, sometimes deeply sad. Often we try reasoning with our feelings, or we reassure ourselves by concentrating on our blessings. We comfort ourselves with food and sneak to movies in the afternoon.

Sometimes we hide our depression in the metaphors of poetry.

### Siren's Song

*I cry in the bathtub.*
*This toxic waste mixes*
*With the undertow beneath my back.*
*A tidal wave forms*
*Between my scissoring legs,*
*Lapping at the shore of my body.*
*The soap, floating free*
*And easy to my reach*
*Slips*
*Like a whale might*
*In another ocean.*
*In the shallows*
*My feet and nipples are bathed*
*In sea-breeze.*
*My hair seaweeds out as I sink.*
*It's quiet below;*
*Only the faint clicking of shrimp*
*And dolphins whistling*
*In the distance.*
*Fish passing by open their mouths*
*In a song too soft for me to hear.*
*Overhead I see the faint outline*
*Of a ship*
*wrecked at sea.*

—Bonnie S. Bostrom

Many of us have great difficulty with unstructured time. This is particularly true of women who are adept at multi-tasking. We are successful because we have been able to juggle many things at once, and when the juggling is not driven by the necessity of the workplace, we begin to have doubts about the importance of our actions, doubts about our own worth. Even people in the counseling profession find themselves before the mirror of self-criticism.

 I lacked faith in myself and had feelings of hopelessness about the future. I began to look back on my life and feel I hadn't accomplished anything. When I was working, I felt that I was accomplishing something every day. Now I was in a place of emptiness. It was depression, and I was paralyzed. I kept

asking myself why I couldn't get out of it. What about all my techniques as a therapist? What about all my advice to everyone else?

After going through all the work of becoming a professional, and
learning to love and appreciate myself, I felt shame. I felt old and ugly
and ashamed. I had no reference, no model. I'm not a little old lady
with curly white hair who can be satisfied with housework and grandchildren. Sometimes I wish I were.

But I don't even believe such women exist. Such women have
grandchildren who are strung out and children who are exhausted
from trying to follow the path we carved out. The perfect woman:
successful, professional and beautiful. I feel like an imposter.

> —*Carol McDermott, M.A., Licensed Professional Counselor and*
> *National Board Certified Hypnotherapist*
> *Mystic, Connecticut*

Shame results from failing the expectations we have for
ourselves. Many women have a tendency to set their expectations very high, to idealize what they consider to be acceptable behavior. If we have done our work well, it only
seems reasonable that we will do our retirement well. Our
culture teaches that retirement is the candy, the dessert after
a very long meal. If we get depressed instead of excited, feel
numb rather than energized, long to go back to work instead
of picking up new interests and hobbies, we wonder, "What
is wrong with me?" Every time the idealized version of how
we *should* feel and act conflicts with the reality of how we
*do* feel and act, our feelings of self-worth are likely to decrease. With this lowered perception of worth comes shame.
We feel something is gone, but what? What fed us so deeply
that we now feel starved, cut off, and totally confused by the
complexity of these emotions?

The hours that we once spent in measured increments
throughout the workday can seem endless when we are left
alone to our own devices with no one urging us to adhere to
a preset schedule. Time is a precious commodity while we
are working. There never seems to be enough time in the day
to accomplish everything that is required of us. We are on
fast forward all the time. Once retired, many of us are faced

with unlimited time. If we aren't at ease with this abundance, anxiety may guide our decision making. We frantically try to fill our days with activities that tire us out, but overall mean little. Some of us respond by becoming immobilized.

We become prey to depression and feelings of worthlessness, emptiness. The problem with being in this new, empty space is that we are alone, perhaps for the first time in our lives. To those of us who have balanced family, career, and countless other demands, being alone with oneself is a new and often terrifying concept.

How wonderful for women who are unafraid of confronting themselves and who see this new space as an opportunity to attach, or reattach, to parts of themselves that were lost, or never found. But many women are truly petrified that the person they know themselves to be will disappear in this new space.

 The only thing that compared with leaving my job as a high school teacher was becoming divorced thirty years ago. It was the early 1970s and I had married a young man from a prominent family. For a woman to work at all in those days was revolutionary, so the idea was for me to teach for two or three years. Then I was expected to quit, have children, join the junior league and be sustained by home and family. So while my husband finished his law degree, I began teaching.

We had no children, and I started falling in love with my profession. This was acceptable to my husband as long as his needs were met: dinner on the table, housework done. My husband's profession created social demands, and I kept the household going in addition to fulltime teaching. That was how it was in those days—the woman had the major responsibility for the home and children and was expected to help advance her husband's career.

We adopted. I took a couple of weeks off when we got the baby and then went back to work. After awhile our social life and my role within the marriage were no longer enough for me. It was my idea to get the divorce, and it created a terrible void, but I still had my work so it wasn't the destitute void I felt when I retired. With work, things felt normal. School had structure and I loved it. I had been in school since I was four years old. My life had a rhythm and a schedule that I depended upon.

After a time I married a fellow teacher. We have a wonderful relationship and a blended family, with my son and his four daughters. He retired before I did and enjoyed it so much that he was convinced I would, too. Instead of planning everything around my school schedule, we wanted to travel during the off-season when it would be less expensive and more leisurely. My husband kept talking about going to Greece and Italy. Friends urged me to retire, describing how wonderful it would be to do the things I'd never had time for. What they didn't understand was that they were imagining themselves, not me. A friend showed me her calendar, packed with activities and appointments, and assured me that my life would be like that as well. That's not what happened.

I put off retiring for three more years. Then, in fairness to my husband, I set the date for the year 2000.

I had been at the same school for so many years, I was now teaching the children of children I had taught. I had even taught my son and all four of my stepdaughters. My classroom was an integral part of my family and a very rewarding part of my life. I developed a team-teaching program that was recognized throughout the state, and in 1987 received a distinguished teacher award.

When I announced my pending retirement, everyone was excited. The parties started in January and I was caught up in a whirlwind of wonderful events. I was the keynote speaker at graduation exercises and received a standing ovation. Over a hundred people attended my retirement party. The mayor of Albuquerque even issued a proclamation declaring May 26, 2000, Carol Tennin Hoffman Day. I was riding the crest of a wave.

School let out and summer came. Summer is usually a lazy time for teachers, a time to recuperate and rest, which I did just like always. Then it was the fall and everyone went back to work. Everyone but me. I went on a trip to Mexico with my mother. Then my husband and I traveled to Greece and Italy, went island hopping and drove the hill towns of Tuscany. The momentum and excitement allowed me to avoid the inevitable day of reckoning.

When the travel came to an end, I was the most desolate person in the world. I had to face what I had been avoiding: my old school. I couldn't go down the street toward the school without crying. I had to take a different route just to go to the grocery store. It seems like I wept every day for months.

My husband is very athletic, plays golf, and does volunteer work. Right now I don't want to volunteer and I don't play golf. Reading used to be a luxury when I could steal a little time for it. Now reading is the object of the day.

Life isn't just about filling up time. There has to be a consequence to how time is spent. There has to be meaning.

I know I am angry because I can't come up with something meaningful to replace my career. I'm angry because I am a take-charge kind of person who is used to calling the shots, yet I'm not handling this very well. I can't blame others. It was my own decision to retire. I'm dealing with this situation intellectually, but the emotional content is difficult. I can see how the anger could become destructive. It's really a kind of despair. A year has passed and I still feel hugely wounded, like I've been cut away from my life source. I gave myself a year to find new meaning and it just hasn't happened.

These days I seem to be making deals with myself. As the result of a fall last November, I'm scheduled to have oral surgery. They will need to wire my jaws shut. I couldn't have done that if I were still teaching. We are going on a chance-of-a-lifetime, fifty-two day cruise around South America. I couldn't have done that if I were still teaching. I am considering taking training to work in a natural history museum and teach children about dinosaurs and such.

Many people won't understand what I'm experiencing. If they are still working and hate it, they will envy me. If they are working and love it, they probably can't imagine how they will feel when they leave. If they are retired and love it, they won't understand what I'm going through. People will think I'm ungrateful and have a great life. I do. We are fortunate to have all our children and eleven grandchildren here in the same town. I have a wonderful husband and my health is good.

I had all those things before I retired and they were a tremendous part of my life, but they can't replace what I lost. What I no longer have is the personal satisfaction and reinforcement that comes from being a teacher. I believe that the role of teacher is a great calling, one that I answered. It is still calling and I'm in grief because I gave it up.

*—Carol Hoffman, M.A., Secondary Teacher, Social Studies*
*Albuquerque Public Schools*

We think we know ourselves well and that we can predict our own behavior. The complexity of our emotions can surprise us.

 Grief and sadness—these weren't the emotions I expected. I was caught off-guard. I had always prided myself in being a woman who jumped up every morning to face the day with vitality and great enthusiasm. I loved my life, my work, my success and my accomplishments. I'm a naturally gregarious, social person. The depression was so insidious that I don't believe I noticed it. I ignored it. After a few weeks things were not going well.

I was staying in bed until nine or ten in the morning. I didn't feel like talking to anyone, not even my husband who seemed distant, even though his office was in our home. His activity seemed a harsh counterpoint to my lack of engagement. I could hear him in his office, planning, talking with clients—working. I was angry. I wanted him to stop everything and just be with me, because I felt terribly alone.

The depression started to take over. I was staying in bed longer and any attempt to meditate put me to sleep immediately. I was sleeping for almost two hours in the afternoon and was not even getting up until after nine. I didn't care how I looked and it didn't matter what day it was. They were all the same. Gray.

Friends were unavailable, since they were all still working. My husband maintained his disciplined routine, working in his office. So there I was with myself on my hands—and I didn't like it.

I phoned friends in the evenings, but was unable to tell them how I felt. I lied and said things were fine, that I loved not having to go to work. Underneath the depression I was beginning to feel shame. I felt ashamed that I wasn't doing anything, wasn't producing anything, and had nothing to show for my time except tidy closets and polished furniture.

Strangely, I couldn't cry. It was as though everything inside would break, shatter into pieces, if I gave my feelings a voice. I became very quiet, which is not like me.

—*Bonnie S. Bostrom*

Women in transition find their thoughts fraught with dim fears, sudden longings for freedom from old constraints, habits of work and concerns about the future. Anxiety and panic attacks are all too common.

The thought of picking out the date for my retirement sent me into a panic. I had kept the relationship vague by telling myself that I would retire within three to five years.

Thinking about retirement made me realize I no longer had years to go, and still had projects to complete.

I had to stop talking about retirement to the administrative staff, because it made them apprehensive and nervous. They seemed to think that the information was too personal, too intimate, and they didn't want to hear about it. It was as though I was letting them down.

Talking about retirement took my focus away from work and made me want to quit and paint. I had been on sabbatical leave for eight weeks and found, to my surprise, that I enjoyed not going to work. During those eight weeks I dealt with the self-imposed mythology that I was incapable of being alone. That fear was wrapped up in concerns about dealing with unstructured time. Since joining the work force in 1985, I had never spent an entire day in guiltless reading. I had stayed up late to read, yes, but had never taken a day off to read. I took a Saturday off recently and read all day long, guilt free.

During the past six years, I have been integrating the professional with the domestic person. I have started to become one person instead of many. I've been restructuring around an empty nest and have more time for myself. My life has a smoother flow and I have time to concentrate on the spiritual dimensions of my life.

When I cast forward and think what my life will be, I become very interested in how others are handling retirement. Most people I know who have retired from this university start looking younger after about a year. They look rested, happy, and are doing such things as taking online courses and building labyrinths in their backyards. Many say they did not realize how good it would be, how much fun. I like to hear that talk.

The academic environment, because it is hierarchical and insular, can be very negative. I have learned to revisit the obstacles before me, to say yes to possibilities, even those that didn't work in the past, and to continue looking for ways to make them work. I spent a lot of time removing barriers that weren't there in the first place, and submitted to my fears of authority when all the while higher administration wasn't paying that much attention to me. My obstacles were self-created and self-imposed.

I'm in mental transition now, preparing to retire. I intend to live my beliefs and apply these beliefs in retirement. Life has more continuity without the work-home schism. I'm more relaxed and enjoy my work now more than before. This sense of continuity has allowed me to begin embracing the idea of retirement instead of going into a panic over it. I've been doing a retrospective on my work life instead of thinking about retirement. That's the magnetic quality of work—it draws you in.

The picture wouldn't be complete without mentioning that I am constructing my retirement speech. I'm thinking about picking and choosing things to talk about that illustrate what I do that people aren't really aware of. Some may remember me for this library building, but that isn't the fullness of my work. I've been working here for thirty-five years and much of what I have done as the dean and director of the library is invisible, but profoundly meaningful to me.

Part of my fear of retirement and aging is fear of losing my partner, who is twelve years older than I. So I am looking forward to spending time with him. I don't have to worry about finances because I've done good financial planning.

I intend to buy myself a chaise lounge. I dream about it. In my dream a lamp emerges from my chaise lounge, which sits in a room filled with books. I don't have a plan for my leisure time. That's sort of an alien concept, but I can easily envision days following one after another. I will take art classes and I will rest on my chaise lounge and read.

Painting is not a replacement for work. It embodies my search for a larger message from the universe. It's like a monk whirling a prayer wheel. It's mixing the paint, putting it on canvas, letting go of thoughts and connecting with other things. That's my destination when I'm no longer bound by work.

—*Jean Collins, M.A., Dean and Director of Library Services, Northern Arizona University*

The incredible sadness and loss we feel are to be expected. So is the fear. We may not have anticipated them, but we must now accept that they will accompany us in our transition out of the workplace, and that they are normal reactions to loss.

It seems remarkable that months have gone by since I left my position. It isn't such a short time, or such a long time, nor is it parsed out in units. I sense time far differently—merely as duration, without clear lines demarcating one month from the next. I frequently don't know what day it is and idly wonder if this is a sign of incipient Alzheimer's. I don't really think it is. Like old telephone numbers that quickly disappear from memory when no longer needed, days vanish because I no longer need to keep track of them. Of course, when I'm expected to be someplace I set my anchor down on the appointed day and hold it there until the event or activity takes place. I keep telling myself that I am not depressed.

Just this week I dreamed about getting a job. When I woke, the dream lingered and I found myself going over the classifieds as though I were hot on the trail, looking for work. I'm not looking for work, but it was a good two days before I stopped actively thinking of getting my resume together, organizing my wardrobe. Part of me is still toying with the idea.

I'm not sure if I keep thinking about getting a job because that's my intention, or because I feel somewhat untethered. Seven months have passed and it seems like something within me should have become solid by now—that the vacant place should have filled.

I've moved to a different state, a new home with new neighbors. I've redecorated, installed hardwood floors, done some landscaping and only today arranged for a completely new heating and air conditioning unit. All very important stuff—all singularly unfulfilling.

If I can define what I want, then perhaps I can get it, or at least understand this constant desire for engagement. I want to be thoroughly engaged. I want all parts of me to be involved in my life. I want active intellectual stimulation and problem solving. Action! I want action. This must be how a gambler feels looking for a game.

It occurs to me that I may have been a workaholic and that what I'm feeling is massive withdrawal from my addiction to work and working too hard. "Too hard" isn't really the right descriptor, "too consuming" is closer. I was consumed by my work. Now I am looking in the mirror, searching to find my reflection, to see what remains. Is there any part of me that was not consumed—not burned up and burned out?

Working was good for me while I was working. But if it was really that good for me, why don't I feel fine without it? Leaving the workplace is like getting off an addictive drug. My emotions swing from despair to elation, from anger to incredulity, and often there is no way to predict which emotion will come next or what will provoke it. I listen to my self-talk and work at giving myself encouragement and positive affirmations. None of it seems to penetrate my defenses. I sense on a deep level that I have been cheated, that something didn't happen that should have. Challenging though it was, my job did not challenge me holistically. The person I thought I was was an illusion. This illusory person still wakes me up some mornings and beckons me back into the dream of what used to be and, in some true sense, never really was.

—*Bonnie S. Bostrom*

Our generation of women has been strong, powerful and comfortable in the world. When retirement devastates us, we don't readily understand what is happening. We are in a new place with few role models to teach us how to behave, how to discover our true selves and how to feel comfortable with those discoveries. We are truly in uncharted territory fighting dragons we never imagined.

## Alien

I am not at home on Earth.
The night sky should look familiar;
the sun would not burn eyes
born of this system.
The praying mantis, moose and crocodile
could be close friends
if I shared with them earth's design.
I resign myself to displacement
and longing
as I view unreadable trees,
and am confounded by the road
from seed to flower.
In exile I wait,
hoping in some way
to make passage home.

—Bonnie S. Bostrom

# Seeking a New Reflection
## Accounts of Successful Transitions

A popular adage says that the fish is the last to see the water. That's how it can be with models, patterns that we perceive dimly, or begin to see as they play out repeatedly in our lives and become second nature to us. We need to step back to recognize, and take the time to honor, those who have influenced our lives. Everyone has a favorite teacher, or a valued mentor.

Even when we have only faint notions of what we will be doing after retirement, we look for signposts. We try to gauge how we will behave by looking at how others do it, how they transition, how they feel about themselves. We talk to our mentors and share with each other.

 When I first came to Santa Fe I had no idea what I would be doing or how I would use my brand new Ph.D. I was put in touch with a wonderful woman named Phyllis Nye who gave me my first work assignment: to travel across New Mexico doing program reviews at early childhood facilities and providing child-abuse prevention training to childcare providers and parents. It is through this assignment that I learned how passion is transformed into action. Phyllis believed in early childhood education and advocated tirelessly for quality. She refused to compromise her ethics or her belief that the teachers who work with young children must be the best trained and most compassionate. I use the past tense because Phyllis died a few weeks ago.

She was not feeling very well and had twice postponed a lunch date to further discuss her contribution to this book. My agenda was not only to obtain her entry, but to talk about how poorly I was handling retirement—even the *word* retirement. I always saw Phyllis as my mentor and thought maybe she could guide me through this process. We never had lunch, but when she died I suddenly felt inhabited by her essence, as though her light had come into my heart and rested there.

At her funeral I saw people I had not seen for years, all involved in the professional service of children. We began to talk about some of the projects that Phyllis was working on just before her death. She was completing a grant for an early-childhood literacy project, even as her daughter drove her to the hospital where she was diagnosed with an aggressive cancer. Her body never left the hospital, but clearly her spirit was very much present. We talked about reconnecting and pulling together our professional expertise to continue the work Phyllis found so important. Often the well-intentioned plans of grieving friends are less practical than therapeutic, but in this case I believe Phyllis' light will guide us to some very important outcomes.

Phyllis' daughter remarked that contributing to this book was very important to Phyllis. She hoped to find her mother's writing among her education journals, novels, music and cooking notes. About a week later it came in the mail. After reading it, I realized the importance of viewing retirement as a developmental process with more and more room for expansion. Phyllis never thought about contraction. She focused on her ideas, her contributions, her energy and the challenge of learning new and exciting things.

The idea that retirement and death are somehow linked is a legacy left to us by our parents, whose lives seemed to end when work ended. This happened to my father as well as to Phyllis' father. Both men retired and became lifeless until their physical deaths.

What actually changed for Phyllis and others of us who say we are retired? What exactly are we retired from? If we used another word like "change" or "expansion" would we feel differently? Like Phyllis, I am doing much of what I did before I retired. It seems that the key is not to do something different, or to do "nothing in particular," but to approach our activities differently. Phyllis exhibited a new kind of excitement. She was able to make choices and did not have to put up with people, rules or demands that sidetracked her from what she believed to be important. Unlike an employee, Phyllis no longer had to compromise. Her passion, her compassion, her willingness to risk in the service of her ideas now had a supportive container.

The fact that Phyllis died as she was writing a grant dispels the idea that the in-basket will be empty when we leave the planet. There will always be things left undone and dreams not fully realized. I have learned the importance of keeping the in-basket full of meaningful activities, and I have learned to put no time limits on dreams. We can dream of possibilities until the very end. Maybe Phyllis is still dreaming, only now she dreams through those of us left to carry her passion forward.

—*Barbara Reider*

Our mentors become part of us as we incorporate their advice, their wisdom and their nurturance. What follows is Phyllis Nye's last writing. You can tell from her words that work was very much her world. We can appreciate her sharing with us these thoughts, made all the more special because they give us a glimpse of someone who touched others, who made a difference in work and in retirement.

 Retirement was a fearful word as far as I was concerned. My father died within two months of his retirement and I felt there was a relationship between retirement and death.

I put this dreadful retirement off as long as possible, however a change in the administration gave me the final push and I "bit the bullet" and retired. I was lucky though: I found a part-time position that was perfect. A dear friend had a vision for an early-childhood program that was a perfect fit. For several years, I considered myself semi-retired and enjoyed every minute. I had ample time for myself and still was productive in an area of education I loved.

Ben Shayn, the artist, once said, "Open new doors all through life," and that is exactly what happened to me—a new door opened.

Art museums always fascinated me. Growing up in New York, it was the Metropolitan. Wonderful afternoons at the Met are fond memories. When my children were school age, we read aloud the book, *The Mixed-Up Files of Mrs. Basil P. Frankweler,* and I would tell them about my memories of the Metropolitan Museum.

After moving to Santa Fe we explored the museums, and I fell in love with the fine arts museum. The building is a special space. It has a certain calm and charming atmosphere with an enchanting court-yard. Well, lo and behold, docent training started there the very week I "retired." How perfect for me! A new door opened, with wonders inside, and I became re-involved in the field I loved.

I even found time to read the newspaper with breakfast, all the professional journals I had neglected, and novels. Imagine reading a novel on a weekday afternoon!

The docent program not only kept me aware of contemporary artists and the changing exhibits that were new and exciting, it al-lowed me to make new friends of various ages and backgrounds, with interesting experiences and ideas. They, in addition, had time to visit, explore and listen, as many were also retired.

Very recently another change occurred. The community college where I taught adopted ideas and a philosophy that no longer suited me. At first I was upset, however now I have more time for me. I don't have to teach evening classes. Cold winter nights are a new joy for me. I don't have to go out; I can remain in my cozy, warm house.

As we grow and age, our needs and interests grow as well. We find new and deeper joys in the simple things we took for granted. There is time to pursue new interests, use libraries, wander through museums and look with new eyes. One afternoon I found myself in the midst of a group of accomplished artists. There I was, bravely drawing at a five-year-old level, and it didn't bother me.

I never thought I would get involved with politics, but guess what? I have time now, and find it interesting and very exciting (especially if the person I support gets the vote).

One of my new delights is having leisurely lunches with people I like. Slow lunches are so much more pleasant. Often we are the only persons remaining in the restaurant.

—*Phyllis Nye, former teacher, mentor, friend*
*Santa Fe, New Mexico*

We are models for women who will face this part of life long after we have gone through it and beyond. Whether we move through this transition with ease or difficulty, younger women will look to us to define the experience.

The work world of men was our model, and what we saw was frightening in many ways. The message we got was that men frequently retired and died. Heart attack and stroke were almost inevitable. Fortunately this is changing for men, and women are finding new ways to view this life passage.

 I graduated from UCLA in 1956 with a degree in business administration. I met my husband of forty-six years while in school. We married right after college and he was either going to be drafted or go to law school. It was the latter, fortunately. As a 1950s woman, I was to be a helpmate to my husband, work to support his schooling and raise our children. His career had priority.

After graduating from college, I took a position as assistant to the executive director of a men's apparel promotion association. Occasionally certain members of the association affectionately patted my behind as I went about my duties. I did not protest at the time. I did not want to cause trouble for myself. Although I stepped into my boss' job when he was out of town, I could never have moved up to his position. I could only remain his assistant.

I realized that, as a young female, albeit well educated, there was no place for me to go in the male-dominated business world. I did not want to be a stereotypical nurse or secretary. The careers that remained were in the teaching field. I returned to night school to get my teaching credential while working during the day. My husband went to law school at night and worked also. I taught off and on for ten years while raising our four children. My husband was very involved in his career, thus child-rearing and home became my responsibilities, along with my teaching duties.

My father was a very positive force in my life and had a lot to do with the decisions I made about career and family. He believed that I could be whatever I chose. My mother suffered from mental illness and was an uninspiring role model. I had many family responsibilities during my childhood.

In 1973, at age thirty-seven, I became dissatisfied with teaching as a lifelong career. Few options were available to former teachers without additional education. My husband suggested that I return to school to become a paralegal. My husband's law clerk discouraged me, suggesting that I was too smart to be, as he put it, a glorified secretary. He told me I should go to law school and become a lawyer. What a terrific idea!

I had recently read Betty Friedan's, *The Feminine Mystique* and concluded that I had the right to pursue the career of my choosing. I informed my husband that his clothes would still be washed, the children cared for and dinner served as usual.

While studying for my bar exam, I moved out of my home and away from household responsibilities for one month. I had evolved from a meek little woman to an assertive person who recognized her right to a life. I passed the bar exam the first time.

I wanted to seek my own career path in the public sector, although I could have worked as my husband's assistant. I took a position as a deputy state attorney for the State of California and became a litigator until I retired almost twenty years later. I was treated fairly and given equal opportunities to advance and grow.

As a lawyer, my social status rose, particularly among males. When I attended parties I was now accepted when I preferred to join male conversations. I always wanted to be seen first as a person and second as a lawyer. I wanted the mirror of society to reflect the real me, but unfortunately the mirror determines your worth by what you do for a living.

Shortly after I retired at age sixty, my husband (who is still working) and I moved from Los Angeles to Santa Fe. After raising our family and pursuing a challenging, rewarding career, I find this present phase the most satisfying. I believe this is because I made the decision long ago to become my own person. When we started our new life in New Mexico, I wondered who I would now be and what I would do with my time. I had always been moving toward some external goal.

My hair started falling out because my body was undergoing an adjustment as well. The thought of watching soaps all day was not enticing, so I made new friends, joined the American Association of University Women and found some wonderful members in my community. I had time to read for fun, play golf, join book and investment clubs, and take classes, but it was not enough. I wanted to give something back to my community. After hearing about Court Appointed Special Advocates for abused and neglected children, a national volunteer organization, I decided to get involved. This has been an emotionally rewarding experience.

Several months ago I had a scare—a minor heart attack. This reminded me of the fragility of life, my life! I really stopped to think about the choices I had made. I was very pleased with myself.

I want other women to know that it is never too late to pursue their dreams. We bring to our retirement phase of life the same values we brought to the earlier phases. For me it is a love of people, continued growth, and the joy of learning.

I really hate the word "retirement." I envision the old folks sitting in rocking chairs on the front porch, watching life go by. It took me about one year to adjust to this new phase of life after living in the gainfully employed world for so long. That year was a sort of grieving process. I retired one month and moved to another state and "state" two weeks later! There was really no time to make a transition from one life to the next. I have also come to realize that retirement means I do not have to do anything I don't want to do. I can make choices. There are no more ought to's or should's. I love it!

—*Beverly Saltz, former Deputy State Attorney, State of California*

A great many women haven't had the opportunity to look closely at women models. Their fathers were the only working parent. Generally, we think of our parents as models when we are young and at home, being raised by them. Yet we are watching them all our lives.

 When I told my daughter that I was considering retirement, she had two responses. One response was to compare me to my father, whose life stopped when he retired. The second was that maybe I could finally figure out why I always seemed to be in motion, why I always gave the impression that "a monkey was chasing me." She suggested that I take some time to be with myself. She astutely recognized that work had kept me away from the very kind of self-reflection she thought important.

My daughter bought me a journal. She was not the only one who thought this would be a good retirement gift for me. I guess it was obvious to more than my daughter that the last person I wanted to get to know was myself. It was evident from talking with my daughter that her observations of my relationship to work were pretty accurate. She recognized how I used work to distance myself from others, including her.

I had waited only two months after my daughter was born to find part-time employment. When she was nine months old I returned to work full time. Since I was involved in an early childhood program, I convinced myself that as soon as my daughter was toilet trained she could attend the program where I worked. She stayed with a neighbor woman until she was ready for preschool. I talked myself into believing that this was a good experience for her, as the neighbor was a loving woman with an extended family of brothers and sisters.

I missed my daughter's first steps, first words, first everything. The babysitter got them all. I, however, had an important job. I felt secure and knowledgeable at the workplace, and totally incompetent as a new mother. I was not at all interested in examining these issues, nor was I interested in examining my marriage. I worked! When my daughter finally joined me at my place of employment, I was in charge of most of the program. My job was time consuming and often kept me at the school late into the evening. My daughter, occupied with toys and fast food, waited for Mom. To be available, both physically and emotionally, would have required that I face myself and my life. I preferred to work and disconnect from any role that might awaken my insecurities.

My father was my role model for work. He was rarely home. He preferred visiting with customers to spending time with his kids. He was a good provider and often remarked at how hard he worked to give us the comforts we had as a family. I remember wishing that I had fewer material things and more of him.

I don't recall Dad putting work second to anything. My mother was a college graduate who stayed home, but never seemed to enjoy being there. One could say they were both stuck in their roles, but if my mom could have worked outside the home I'm not sure she would have. The legacy that I received from my parents was simply that working outside the home was of greater value and more meaningful than being a parent and family member. I am sure I did a very good job of communicating the same message to my daughter.

Fortunately, my daughter and I can have the kind of conversation that could break this cycle. She understands how I used work and also how my father used work. Work was where we felt successful. It was also where we could construct relationships the way we wanted them to be. We did not have to worry about real connection, real reciprocity. The demands of work were considerably fewer and more controllable than the relationship of parent to child. My daughter understands now that I was hiding from me, not from her, but I am sure she felt negated throughout her childhood, as I did throughout mine.

I hope that I can serve as a model in retirement. I have been trying to let my daughter know that being with myself is becoming more and more comfortable. I am trying to let her know that balance is important and that it is safe to construct relationships outside the workplace. Outside relationships take more honesty and a willingness to embrace equality, but they are deeply meaningful and fulfilling. I want her to understand that if I had to do it again, I would work, but I would also work for balance. I do not advocate using work as a place to hide from oneself. I want her to know that the "monkey" is no longer in control.

I am glad for the work that I have done and still do, and that I am successful and have many professional achievements. I guess in some ways I am doing it again, only with a different consciousness. I am modeling that I can work, but in addition have time to think, reflect, and build relationships. I hope she sees a positive model that she can use before she is ready to say the word, "retire."

—*Barbara Reider*

In the book, *Goddesses in Everywoman*, Jean Shinoda Bolen talks about the warrior Athena as a dominant archetype for some women. As warriors and strategists, women following this model are too involved in school or work to develop other aspects of their lives. Bolen points out that these women find it difficult to see that their competitive involvement in the marketplace, political arena, or academia comes at a high price. Intense focus on a career can arrest emotional development and limit intimate relationships. In addition, intensely career-driven women may have little inner life and a dearth of simple pleasures and spontaneous moments, qualities that go unnoticed until the woman slows down.

Change and growth come to an Athena if life forces her to shift perspective and open her heart. Painful as this may be, with losses strong enough to penetrate the woman's intellectual armor, it may facilitate introspection and openness to feelings of grief, vulnerability and loneliness. Healing can begin once we empty out the hurt. We replace deprivation, loss and isolation through association with others and a deeper connection to ourselves.

 I first noticed women leaving home to work during World War II. Prior to the war, my mom was there anytime we were. Later, my brother and I were left to ourselves much of the time. I noticed, too, that my mom and dad were arguing more and were very tired. They paid for me to take piano lessons and then didn't want to hear me practice. I could see that, with the paycheck, women had the power of decision, unless of course they gave the money to the man of the house. This caused some disgruntled feelings.

My mother had a tenth-grade education. After the divorce, in 1945, she worked at anything she could find. When I was going to high school she worked in a shoe factory and waited on tables during lunch, the latter buying the three of us a good, hot midday meal.

Mother worked very hard until she remarried in 1950 to a wealthy farmer. She made friends in the community and loved playing cards and visiting with her sister, who lived nearby. My aunt was the wife of a mortician and a registered nurse. I cleaned house and baby-sat for her and I could see that she was well respected in the city where she and her husband lived. My Mom was from a family of nine children, so getting along with people came to her quite naturally.

Why do I tell you so much about my mother's life? Whether I like it or not, she shaped my life by the things she did and didn't do. I never felt that I was her friend—sometimes not even her daughter. She had beautiful naturally curly hair, smooth skin and was desirably plump. I was the opposite. She didn't know what I was about, and when I tried to talk to her she would say, "I just don't understand you." I wrote a poem about her.

*Mother*
*Black eyes in a moon face*
*Surrounded by a sea of black wavy hair,*
*A beauty in her prime,*
*Loved the attention given her*
*And was caught up*
*In a patriarchal society of women who were made to work.*
*Angered by her father and by her first husband*
*Who used her,*
*She had a motto, often repeated,*
*"It's as easy to love a rich man as a poor man."*
*Prophesy, as prophecies do,*
*Materialized.*
*She became a woman of money*
*Was confused over affection and money,*
*Gave money instead of affection,*
*Added to the confusion of all.*
*If I take her affection*
*Does it mean that my love can be bought?*
*How much more powerful*
*I would have felt*
*If she had looked at me and said,*
*"I admire you for your love of me,*
*Your strength,*
*Character,*
*And your abilities."*
*But, alas,*
*I have had to say these things to myself*
*But, in this,*
*I truly have authenticity.*
*Aged now, but always the beauty, she asks,*
*"How old do you think I am?"*
*The surprise and giddiness follow,*
*always self-directed attention.*
*I smile and silently scream, "See me, see me!!!"*

I worked for two years at a dead-end job for the State of Missouri and then decided to go to nursing school. After graduating in 1950, I married and my husband and I moved. At that time Houston was the "hot spot," offering a lot of opportunity. My husband arranged a transfer and I got a job as a recovery-room nurse at Methodist Hospital, where leading heart surgeons Michael DeBakey and Denton Cooley practiced. I chose recovery in order to get weekends off, important in a new relationship. My career was stable for two years. Then I took time off for my first child and stayed home until money pressures sent me back to work part-time.

Once my two daughters were in school I worked as the director of emergency services at a large hospital, where I managed a staff of thirty nurses and was totally responsible for patient care around the clock. This job interfaced with the community and also with the newly developing Emergency Department Nurses Association of which I became the national secretary.

Nursing in the 1950s was in flux. Young women went into the profession to take care of people, so when I was released from my leadership position I went back to caring for patients. I missed the money, but enjoyed the feeling of being appreciated.

I've accomplished a lot in my life. When I married for the second time at forty-five, I began an entirely new life. My husband was an engineer and loved to fly. We bought a small plane and I took flying lessons. I became a real estate agent and pursued a sales career for six years. I took care of my father-in-law for two years in our home. Later, I spent two years caring for my mother. There is little I would change about that time. I loved that I was a nurse and could care for them. Later, when I developed an electrical defect in the nodes in my heart and was medicated with blockers and a pacemaker, it was helpful to know what was going on in my body. Understanding erases fear.

I have served as president of many organizations, belong to art and bridge groups and am active in my community. I have never felt a loss of power or an absence of things to do. All I need do is pick up the phone and volunteer, or ask for what I want. When one door shuts, an opportunity to do something more interesting usually materializes. I have been at the bottom and the top of the ladder, and have never fallen, thanks to my very carefully developed lateral support system.

> —*Myra Blackburn, former Hospital Administrator; National Secretary, Emergency Department Nurses Association*

An older Athena may be entering into a phase where she receives recognition for her work, mentors others, and is at her most creative.

Many of the women featured in this book could easily be identified as Athenas. For some, leaving the battleground of the workplace forces a change in perspective. Feelings of loss are apparent in the stories women tell about the transitions they experienced. For years the train moves so fast that from the window everything looks great. We do not carve out the time needed to build reciprocal relationships, reflect on our emotions, or recognize  our fears. When time becomes available, it is quickly filled. We nurture a false sense of wellbeing where our needs are met and we are in control. When the train finally stops, unless we are willing to find the tools to become the Athena crone, we feel stuck in depression, believing that we have done our life's work and feeling little excitement for the future.

Retirement may be the opportunity for Athena to examine her life, to add a spiritual dimension to her experiences. Our new life's work can be the continuation of our own development. It can be a time to move from our egos, often disconnected and protected, to being in the world as a mentor and sharer of wisdom.

Once we have grieved the loss of power, control, security and socially constructed work relationships, new forms of exploration are possible. Retirement is potentially a period of significant social change, with women coming together in dialogue and support, as we did during the consciousness-raising era of the 1960s and 70s.

We are living at a time when retirement does not have to mean the end of anything. It can mean the beginning of a new phase of life, one rich in possibilities for growing wisdom and a giving spirit.

## I Am Walking Toward Joy

I am walking toward joy,
The difference now is in the turning home.
You asked me years ago what I want
From my old age; no answers came,
Or too many, the ends of a life
Neatly gathered, to justify
Where I have been, felt, hoped.
Keeping those I love nearby,
An essay, rather than a poem.
This walking, then, is like a prayer,
A conversation full of noticing,
No pantheistic view of nature in soft focus,
No turning from, but walking toward.
Joy comes in the morning,
In your welcoming smile
As we go out,
Gathering.

—Ann Ragsdale

# Dusting Off the Mirror of Dreams
## Taking Risks and Fulfilling Lifelong Aspirations

If we follow our dreams, let spirit guide us and take risks we previously felt incapable of, we give ourselves opportunity. Women are seldom viewed as intrepid adventurers who can spontaneously take off for the Himalayas, or explore other cultures and places we have only read about.

 A graying gypsy hippie roams new territory.
I had feelings of elation and transcendent peace as I left the administration building of the substance-abuse treatment center for the last time. I was retired! I reflected on some of the high points of my life, exploring exotic places on the four corners of the globe and learning spiritual truths from great teachers. I suddenly felt like a kid in a candy store. I could do this all the time!

I have subsequently traveled throughout northern South America, Central America, Spain, and Southeast Asia. What enthralled me most were the Buddhist temples in the hills of northern Thailand and Southwest China. By the time I visited the first temple, I had fallen in love with idyllic Thailand—the exuberant friendliness of the people, leisurely pace, charming customs and beautiful rolling hills blanketed with lush foliage.

With my friend Ping (who adopted me as "Mom"), I climbed 290 steps, flanked by a mythical serpent balustrade, to Wat Doi Suthep at 3,520 feet, overlooking Chiang Mai. At the center of this fourteenth century monastery was a large chedi (spired pagoda) housing several golden Buddha images and relics of the Buddha. The splendor of the hills, multicolored flowers, birds, the monks in saffron robes, bells ringing, and burning incense washed over me. I suddenly felt an overwhelming oneness with all of nature, every living being, and the great Enlightened Ones (Buddha, Krishna, Gandhi, Jesus, and my guru, Swami Brahmananda). I felt a great surge of liberation and envisioned all the pieces of my life's puzzle falling neatly into place.

Ping, aware that I was visibly moved, quietly asked if I would like to light a stick and pray to the Buddha. I fervently prayed for peace in a world recently ravaged by the events of September 11 and its aftermath. I reflected that it was time for us as humans to embrace the compassion of the Buddha.

I was similarly deeply inspired at the Lama Buddhist temple atop Drilliwub's Island on Lugu Lake in Southwest China. In the heart of the original Shangri-La area, the pristine lake is at 10,000 feet, surrounded by lofty mountains, swathed with primeval forest and often covered with clouds. My fellow travelers and I ascended the narrow dirt path to the nineteenth century temple that had been destroyed and rebuilt several times. One soul boy (an incarnation of a Dalai Lama) had been born there. A short, elderly monk invited us to enter the temple to pray or meditate.

As I stepped outside the temple and looked at the light shimmering on the lake below, I felt awe and reverence. There was surely no better place on earth to be! I embraced oneness with the Supreme Being (called by many names), all people in the world (especially the Tibetans) and the peaceful bliss of my true nature. Again, I fell in love, but this time it was with Southwest China.

If the reader wonders whether I have felt continual bliss in retirement, the answer is no. Following my first retirement venture to Central and South America, I felt profound and unshakable boredom. I was greatly tempted to return to the challenging drama of the mental health field. Turning inward for guidance, I was led to seek fulfilling activities and service work. I have subsequently tried my hand as elementary school volunteer, workshop and meditation assistant, discussion-group leader, seminary student, travelogue writer and pupil of great teachers (Jean Houston, Jon Kasbat-Zinn and Caroline Myss). I immerse myself fully in each new activity for a few months, then continue the rewarding ventures and abandon the bland ones. Periodic visits with my daughter and extended family in Manhattan are priorities as well.

I have experienced a few hard knocks in retirement. My sister and I were close, especially following the deaths of our parents, and traveled together throughout Africa in 1998. She later climbed Mounts Kilimanjaro and Aconcagua, the highest peaks in Africa and South America. Her mysterious disappearance (and presumed death) in a national park in August 2000, was a great blow to me. The temptation to work as many hours as possible returned. Instead, I moved steadily through the painful grieving process.

As I slowly re-embraced life, my sister's spirit guided me to travel again. I felt her spirit many times in Thailand and China. The untimeliness of her death reinforced for me the importance of seizing each opportunity to fully and consciously live. In our last hours in this life, we will probably not regret the time we did not spend in the office, but rather, the missed opportunities to live and love fully. So I celebrate my ventures and adventures in retirement.

—*Marilyn Sapsford, M.S.W., former social worker*
*Grand Junction, Colorado*

Dreams sustain us, guide us, and lend a dimension of forward casting to our lives as we build tomorrow out of the dreams of today. We cherish our dreams, at times in secret, and we share them with the ones we love. They may wait for us, hidden deep within, and emerge when we least expect them. As we grow older, we must remember the dreams of our youth and avoid letting go of long cherished aspirations. Too often we discard our dreams, thinking they are impossible to reach, or that it's too late for new adventures. The truth is, all doors should remain wide open.

When President Kennedy first created the Peace Corps, I immediately wanted my husband and I to join. Taking children along was permissible at that time. I felt the experience of living and working in an impoverished country would not only benefit the people we served, but enlighten my family as well. It would afford us the opportunity to reach out in friendship to others, one country to another, and to raise the global consciousness of our two young sons. However, my husband, who was just launching his engineering career, reasoned that the timing was not right. He convinced me to put the idea on hold.

We had long conversations on the subject and finally decided to wait until the boys were away at college. And so the dream was tucked away. Years later after both sons had gone away to school, I reminded my husband of our agreement. By this time we were well traveled and had lived abroad, so he was quite surprised that serving in the Peace Corps was still an important goal for me.

This time my husband reasoned that he was near the pinnacle of his professional life and could not afford to leave. I countered that I was becoming stagnant in my job. I had enjoyed a rewarding, successful career in education, but had decided not to become a principal or advance into administration. I felt I had explored my options and that none seemed to fit the role I was looking for.

I wanted to be nearby when our sons married and had children, and as other family members aged. I argued that our health as we got older might also become a factor.

Finally we agreed that I would join the Peace Corps, but would seek an assignment in a location where my husband could frequently visit. Many offers were forthcoming and the Belize placement was a perfect compromise.

As the time for commitment approached, however, my husband became anxious about the plan and was unable to follow through. Discussions again ensued and, after a long night of reviewing our options, I agreed to relinquish my dream. I never brought up the subject again because I did not want to create any underlying resentment between us. And so the dream was put to sleep.

Several years later, my husband became ill with cancer. After suffering for over two years, he lost the battle. Had I joined the Peace Corps earlier, I'd have missed several of the years we shared, and I'd have had no dream to resurrect. Now I did.

Seeing the "Oh, poor Carolyn" looks in the eyes of my friends was more than I could bear. I did not want my place in life determined by their images of me as a widow. I foresaw endless well-meant platitudes and could not deal with being pitied. I wanted to be seen as me, a vital, worthwhile, strong woman.

Putting my career behind me was not difficult since I had this long unfulfilled goal to look forward to. I didn't want to stay in my old life, in the same surroundings, and become self-absorbed in grieving. So I took a leave of absence and accepted a Peace Corps assignment in Grenada.

None of my friends and associates in the Peace Corps knew me previously. There is no past with which to compare me, so they accept me as a single woman, not as a widowed educator. They look at me as a person beginning a new life, not as one retiring from an old one.

—*Carolyn Jernigan, M.A., Teacher of Gifted and Talented; Peace Corps Volunteer, Grenada*

We can script our lives even as we lay our dreams aside— then act them out later. We can add new scenes and acts. After we have raised children, completed the years required to earn our retirement or pension, buried our loved ones and taken care of everyone else, we still have the luxury of reaching out to claim new territory, climb real mountains and take on new projects.

 My lifestyle choice has been to work part-time and live simply. Recently I checked my social security account, for which I will be eligible in three years, and saw only a small savings. I have also been investing through a stock club in order to learn about investments and prepare for a happy old age.

When I saw the social security balance, I thought it would provide a fine income in a third-world country. This triggered memories of a time when my life was unfettered and I had enough money to travel and live anywhere in the world. For two years my travels took me through southern Europe, the Middle East and Asia.

I have been a student of the spiritual practice of Sufism and have had an unflagging interest in Persian culture—the architecture, philosophy, culture, arts and crafts.

In my musing about where I would like to live, I have identified several criteria. I want to live in a country that values older single females, a country with religious tolerance, Persian cultural elements and a non-authoritarian culture. I hope to set up a trading company and learn the language and culture. My first thought is Turkey, but I shall probably end up in Spain.

My stepfather is a dear man, soon to be ninety and going strong. While I will make reconnaissance trips to check out candidate countries, I'd like to delay the move until after Pop makes his final journey.

I see myself working after retirement. Sometimes I'll get paid for it. At present I am a professional storyteller and oral historian. I will always listen to, collect and tell stories. Perhaps I will live this retirement story!

—JonLee Joseph, M.A., Teacher, *English as a Second Language*

Some of the women who submitted stories while they were still contemplating retirement have contacted us after the fact to share how they are faring. We can take heart from their experiences and glean some helpful themes from their writings. By entering the experience knowing that it may prove difficult, we will not be caught unaware.

One thing is clear. It is important to have a balanced life to begin with. Even if we are still working, finding balance between work and recreation is crucial. If the scales are tipped too far in the direction of work and everything revolves around our career, retirement may send us reeling. Additionally, it is important to build friendships outside the workplace so that when we retire we don't leave all our friends behind.

Some people benefit by relocating to a new state or city. Building a life in a new environment seems to have a rejuvenating effect. If moving is not feasible, it is very important to develop nurturing activities and hobbies that can be pursued during the transition from work to retirement.

Many women are happy taking on different types of projects and accepting part-time work in their chosen fields. They move out of their careers one step at a time. Many also derive satisfaction from mentoring others in their field. And of course more time is available for the type of mindfulness that can lead to self-discovery.

I am more determined than ever to help women make retirement a great time in their lives. I am developing exercises for women to work through when they are contemplating, or already in the throes of, retiring. It's important to me to have projects where I can take what I am experiencing and feeling and turn it into something helpful to others.

I must admit that I am still struggling. I have found that getting to know myself in new ways is not always pleasant. I have denied, repressed and willed away parts of myself. Working as a Hakomi therapist, mostly with women, has helped me to locate parts of myself that I had given up, hidden or rejected. I am reclaiming my "self." Even though this task of self-discovery is not always pleasant, it always seems important. Retirement brings the opportunity to come to grips with all aspects of the self that have been in shadow. It's a time to face that darkness and turn it into creativity.

—*Bonnie S. Bostrom*

Many women have told us that sharing their stories was a great help to them. As Georgeann Raco expressed it, "Holding my story in my hands when I proofed it was very meaningful and helpful. The experience helped me to take an objective look at what I was going through instead of keeping it bottled up inside. It was therapeutic."

We didn't know at the outset how important the women we interviewed, and their stories, would be to our own recovery. It has been especially rewarding to hear from women for whom retirement was very difficult. Recently we got this note from Carol Hoffman, the teacher whose exit from the classroom was accompanied by great sadness and longing.

 After three years of bumbling in the retirement world, I have gone back to work! I draw retirement *and* a full time salary (play money indeed!).

I did everything I was supposed to do: traveled to Australia, South America, Africa, Fiji; became a docent at the museum of natural history, joined two book clubs and went out to lunch. Now I am back in the classroom—not forever, but for awhile and I love it!

Moral: I simply was not ready to retire. Society said I should be, my husband wanted me to be, and I tried to be.

> Now I know the time will come naturally, and I will be able to accept it without kicking and screaming.
> —*Carol Hoffman*

Carol learned from her grief and loss that she must time her transition based on the desires of her own heart, not on the needs of others. When choices are avi.able, we must choose what we truly want. That old adage, "To thine own self be true," must become a banner for women facing this life change. Following one's inner compass is always important, but in this regard it is crucial.

Silvia Almeida, the graphic artist, is doing well. She and her daughter, Sabina, are moving from Stonington to Norwich, Connecticut, where Sabina will be attending the Norwich Academy. Silvia's health is still fragile and she will be going through chemotherapy during the next few weeks. Her health may be fragile, but her spirit is strong. When she called, she was packing their lives into boxes, looking forward with great joy to a new town, a wonderful opportunity for her daughter and renewed, positive anticipation of the future.

JonLee Joseph is still pursuing the adventurous life. We heard this from her:

> I lived and worked in the northeast of Thailand for a year and a half, teaching English at Mahasarakham University. The country, culture and people are kindly and respectful.
>
> I felt I was in heaven. During my stay I marked the deaths of my parents with a Buddhist ceremony, wishing their spirits well on their journey.
>
> Presently, I have decided on a nomadic lifestyle. I'm back in Seattle, visiting dear friends, reviewing stored items and investing funds. My plans are to visit friends on the east coast before going to Ireland to hear stories, then Turkey to pay my respects to Jelaluddin Rumi, and then on to Spain to work and find a place to live a happy old age. I envision settling in a village near Barcelona where the local people outnumber the ex-pats. I love to learn by living in other cultures and by contributing to the wellbeing of a community through my work and relationships.
> —*JonLee Joseph*

Once they get through the throes of change, many women find new aspects of themselves coming to the fore. Their lives take on a different tone, a new texture. Portions of life that were blurred when every moment demanded action now come into richness and clarity. Jean Collins found fullness when she retired from Northern Arizona University. We have this update from her. Apparently, the future she faced with dread is turning out to be wonderful.

 I arrived in Arkansas in the latter part of January. For the first couple of months I was genuinely thrilled to look at the clock early in the morning, realize that I did not have to get up until I jolly well felt like it, and then go back to sleep. It was wonderful to read late into the night, especially one of the many gardening books I brought with me. There were days and days of doing exactly what I wanted.

During the first couple of months, I spent a lot of time assessing how I was feeling about retirement. I watched for signs that I had made a really big mistake. I took my pulse on this issue frequently. But I felt primarily joy, a secret pleasure in having successfully escaped, and a strong conviction that I truly deserve my retirement. I am dedicated to not letting anyone take it from me. I was determined not to fritter away my time on things I didn't want to do. I was not willing to waste my time, not even a minute.

Within weeks I discovered the joy of full awareness—of enjoying each activity for what it was. I could take my time trying new recipes, because that's all I had to concentrate on. When I was at the university, although I didn't notice it at the time, I was always doing one thing in preparation for doing another. I was always getting ready to do something or go somewhere—to a meeting, to work, to finish a report. I had to get chores out of the way—dishes, laundry, housecleaning, cooking. Now, all of a sudden I have time to slow down and actually be present in the moment, rather than spend every moment anticipating the next important activity.

There were many epiphanies the first few months of retirement, many wonderful surprises. Most expectations were met or exceeded. The other shoe didn't fall. No one came and stole my retirement joy. My dream of long and happy hours with my grandson, Kyel, came true. He loves my cooking. He took me to my first 3-D movie. We went to football games at his school, including homecoming. We visit antique stores, nurseries and candle stores.

I live for Kyel's famous one-liners. We were headed to an antique store in Prairie Grove, down a winding two-lane highway and he said, "Grammy, will you tell me as soon as you think we are lost?" The other day, he was helping me in the garden and said, "You don't have to be a rocket scientist to see that I am a genius." A few weeks back we were digging a hole in the back yard to plant some shrubs and severed a sewer pipe. I started laughing and Kyel asked, "Grammy why are you laughing?" I said, "Well, I gotta laugh now, because there's not going to be much chance after we tell your grandpa." In the first few months I had so many epiphanies that my husband, Lee, told me to be careful or I might turn into an "epiphaninny."

I miss the power of my position as Dean. I miss the dynamic relationships, the exciting staff meetings and watching active, bright minds approach and solve problems. I miss the conversations, repartee and humor of my office staff. I miss being in charge. I miss having someone to anticipate my every little computer problem, to hang on my words, to do my bidding, to follow my instructions. I didn't realize that I hadn't actually relinquished my title until I overheard a conversation between my husband and a friend of his. Mike was asking Lee how it was going with me being retired and home all of the time, and I heard Lee say, "It's a bitch. She's gone from having a staff of eighty to a staff of one and that's me." Later when we talked and laughed about it, Lee said, "And don't go calling any staff meeting—I just might not attend."

When I said farewell to the library staff and university friends, I assured everyone that I wouldn't miss the university retirement party, that I would be there in April without fail. When I received the actual invitation in March, I realized that I didn't want to go back for the party, so I didn't. It was that simple. At the time, I didn't realize what a major step that was.

Just a few days after I made that decision, our next-door neighbor decided to sell her house and move to an assisted-living facility. She offered us first choice on the house and adjoining lots. We deliberated very briefly, maybe a couple of days, before we committed to the purchase. I had been so adamant about keeping my home in Arizona and living in both Arkansas and Arizona—the best of all seasons and climates —that Lee's jaw dropped when I said, "Why don't we sell the house in Flagstaff?" I didn't realize until that moment that I'd said goodbye to Flagstaff when I left in January.

Upon reflection, I realize that hanging on to the house in Flagstaff had been my way of hedging my bets, of staying in touch and possibly in control of the library, of not having to say goodbye in any permanent way to my best friend, Jenny. Saying goodbye to Jenny was one of the saddest moments of my life. I cried more that day than I did when my mother died. I couldn't bear being away from Jenny and I comforted myself by believing that I'd be in Flagstaff six months of the year and in Arkansas the other six.

The house sold relatively quickly and I have no regrets, only relief and a lot more money—money to travel back to Flagstaff, or anywhere in the world for that matter. I like being in one home rather than camping in two places. I'm excited about building a greenhouse and a straw-bale studio in spring. I'm looking forward to long, quiet days of painting.

After we bought the house next door, I embarked on a frenzy of domesticity—redecorating, buying furniture and plants, gardening, painting, cleaning, repairing, building walks. Lee hired three hard working college students. Day after day, we all worked our butts off from daylight until dark. They were much younger and could take the hard work, humidity and heat. We were exhausted. It was becoming an ordeal. I remember late one afternoon saying to Lee, "You're just no fun anymore." He said, "Okay, that's it. We're going to Tulsa! Tomorrow!"

When I was working, I talked a lot about how great it would be to live close to Tulsa so we could bop over to the Gilcrease and Philbrook Museums. We went to the magnificent Gilcrease. I slept on the way over and on the way back. I got to revisit the glorious paintings of Thomas Moran. I got my head back on straight. I retired again. I was trying to get the houses, yards and gardens in Arkansas into the same beautiful shape as my garden in Flagstaff had been. It dawned on me that I had been trying to do in one summer what had taken me eighteen years in Flagstaff. After that realization, it felt quite natural to kick back and relax. Lee and I didn't actually talk much about the meltdown, but we both realized coming back from Tulsa that we had to slow down and enjoy our retirement.

I renewed my commitment to protecting his retirement activities as well as my own. I remind myself that I promised to do my fair share of the household chores, chores that Lee had taken care of when I was working fulltime and he was a stay-at-home husband, already retired. We took a four-hour train excursion through the Ozarks to see the fall colors. We drove to Eureka Springs for the day. We go to movies. We'll spend Thanksgiving with our family in Florida and fly to Oregon to be with family for Christmas. The fun part of retirement is a whole lot better since we got back from Tulsa.

When autumn hit and the fall colors were so spectacular, I stood on my Arkansas porch looking out over the Ozarks and was hit with almost overpowering bursts of joy. I thought I would simply explode. My body couldn't contain the beauty, the freedom, the happiness I felt inside.

One expectation has not been met: I haven't completed a painting since I retired. My studio has been cleaned up twice and retrieved from degeneration into a storage space for building and gardening tools. I've continued to tell people that I retired so I could paint, because it's still true. I have no doubt that I will start painting when the weather turns cold and gardening is over until spring, but I think my friends and family get a little antsy about it. To me it's just one of those things that will happen in due time. I'm not worried about it. I have eleven paintings right on the tip of my brain waiting, less patiently every day, to be painted.

—Jean Collins

Retirement can bring surprises, and opportunities to fully experience each and every moment. Jean is taking time to build a new home, new gardens and new relationships, and to savor them to their fullest. Each of us will face our new life in unique ways, given our history, talents and the challenges ahead.

We hear from women who are dabbling in the work they did before retirement. Many women find new ways of being useful once they retire and are free from the consuming commitment of a fulltime career.

When we were young, we read fairy tales and dreamed of who we would become. The stories guided us in some deep inexplicable way. The stories we now share with each other about managing change can be guides as well.

People in transition are straddling two different worlds. Of paramount importance during any period of great upheaval is the ability to traverse unexplored waters. How do we proceed? Some of us breeze through these changes as though running with the wind, not against it. Some women plan for retirement carefully and, because they plan, seem to have very little difficulty adjusting.

Women are resilient. We drag out our bag of tricks and begin trying things. Travel is something many of us hoped to do when we had the time. Planning and incorporating travel, weaving it into our lives, can be richly rewarding.

 My mother thought I would be a good teacher. Now, after a career of twenty-two years, I guess she was right. I retired in 1999. I am still subbing a little at the high school and have been going to school myself. I've taken painting classes and courses to become certified in English as a Second Language. I also studied French and have been to France three times.

One of my goals was to travel in May and September. I've been to Alaska, and a friend and I took a tour of the homes of literary figures in New England—Thoreau, Cather, Frost, Alcott, Emerson.

I really retired to be at home, to work in my garden, paint, complete my family genealogy and, of course, travel. My four children have been very helpful and supportive. They have given me books on travel for women.

I began my journal before I retired, entitling it, "Retirement: Future Think." I wrote this quotation in the front: "One life lies behind, unfilled time lies ahead."

Most retirement books concentrate on money, money, money, so I started my own journal two years before I retired and assembled a list of forty-one things I wanted to do, including changing food habits, keeping up with letter writing and lots of activities to challenge my mind.

I have a great garden—one of the forty-one activities I set for myself—with beds for organic food, flowers and herbs. I have six grape vines, several fruit trees and am adding more all the time. Flowers bloom all year round, though I have an ongoing battle with the deer.

My morning schedule includes studying French, writing at least three pages and painting. The afternoons are free. For years I created daily lesson plans. Now I use a similar kind of planner to schedule my activities. I even have things planned for rainy days.

My training taught me that people are multidimensional, so I provide for my emotional, physical and mental needs.

I need role models, so I ask friends in their eighties and nineties for advice and guidance. One couple swim, play bridge and participate in Elder Hostel. They read the New York Times and can talk on any subject. They are wonderful models.

I'll leave the volunteer work until later when I'm not so busy. Right now I am joyously jobless.

—*Martha Perry, Teacher, Gifted and Talented*
*Groton, Connecticut*

Joyously jobless! Martha's experience illustrates that planning, discipline and follow-through are skills that, when focused on ourselves instead of the workplace, can further our quest for new meaning and happiness. Focusing on our interior life, we can find joy in new and unexpected places.

In the summer of 1992, I reluctantly became a fly fisher. Had I not, the chances of seeing my husband on weekends seemed slim. Over a period of several years, he had fallen in love with fly fishing and had become a skillful and beautiful fisherman. I wasn't much inclined to share his enthusiasm, but did agree to give it a try.

Fishing wasn't so bad, but I knew right away that I lacked the focus and, especially, the patience necessary to enjoy myself. My style is to do ten things at once, switch gears instantaneously, be as quick and efficient as possible and look for immediate and positive feedback. In spite of my lack of enthusiasm, my husband—just like a fly fisher—was patiently and relentlessly trying to hook me.

Around the beginning of December, I started dropping hints that, although I was willing to continue trying, I was not ready to fully commit to fly fishing. My husband's response was, "Too late." My waders, vest, hat, rod, reel and fly box were already safely tucked away for the opening of the season. When I suited up for my first day, I must admit I looked great!

That summer, I tried hard to catch fish, but as predicted my patience for untangling knots in the line wore thin. I had little tolerance for games of tug-of-war with bushes on the opposite bank, or tying perfect knots to attach flies only to have them unravel at the slightest tug. Then one day it happened. I was sitting on a boulder untangling a knot and I heard birds singing and water rushing over the rocks. The air smelled of pine and the sky was that unreal New Mexican blue. I suddenly realized that there was nowhere else I would rather be and nothing I would rather be doing. The light bulb, as they say, went on. Was this what it really was about—slowing down and looking around? Concentrating on one thing at a time and taking the time to focus? Changing my priorities and enjoying the moment?

I am now retired, after a satisfying thirty-two year career. I was somewhat reluctant to become a retiree. I loved the people with whom I worked. I worried about missing their stimulation, whether we would stay in touch and, even worse, losing my place in the gossip loop. I had always worked, and wondered how much of my identity was wrapped up in my job. What would I tell people when they asked what I did, or requested my work phone number? I felt great about my career and what I had accomplished, but wondered if that was enough. Would I feel the need to be productive? And how would I fill the empty hours?

Recently I was in my car when I felt the sudden need to pull off to the side of the road. I had an epiphany—that old light bulb had gone on once again. With a jolt, I realized that now every day is like fly fishing on the river. And so I've slowed down. I look around, converse with folks in the grocery store and go hiking and dog-walking with family and friends. I'm focusing on things I've always wanted to do, but could never fit into my schedule. I'm learning to enjoy the time and freedom to just be. By now I have become a somewhat accomplished fly fisher. For me, catching a fish is not really the point. Catching time is. Soon I hope to be an accomplished retiree.

—*Ellyn Feldman, Co-founder and former Director, Children's Museum of Santa Fe*

Some women are able to leave work and find similar situations that bring great meaning and depth to their lives. They find new ways of becoming useful.

I was told I would fail at retirement! I knew this woman who had cards made up that said, "Retiree." This is what she handed out when she was asked what she did. I could never do that.

My mother and father were both college educated. Dad pressured Mom to give up her women's rights politics, so she put the energy into her kids. I was the youngest, and she decided when I was in kindergarten that I was going to go to medical school. I was in school for thirty-two years—it felt like my entire life.

I was chair of the Psychiatric Department at the University of Minnesota Medical School before retiring, and identify myself as a pioneer. Retirement really did not change the direction my life has taken. I did not have hobbies, so I worried some about what I was going to do when I no longer worked. I'm on a number of editorial boards and continue to attend professional meetings.

I am divorced and have three children and five grandchildren whom I wanted to visit when I stopped working fulltime. I also wanted freedom to travel, which I did the first year. I moved to New Mexico to be closer to my daughter. I like the cultural offerings and the change of seasons in Santa Fe.

I was happy when I first retired. Many of my women friends were not working. I joined some of them on a trip, which required that I learn to hike. That first year was very busy.

I retired to relax and travel, but this did not seem to work after awhile. I missed being on the cutting edge of psychiatry. The activities I planned for retirement were not enough. I began looking for temporary assignments in my field. I was invited to work at the University of New Mexico after volunteering there. As a researcher, I had gained so much knowledge and experience in the clinical aspects of psychiatry, I felt I needed to utilize this information professionally. I now teach, which I really love, and see some patients. My primary interests are research and teaching. I was always a prolific researcher.

When, after twenty years, I decided to leave the University of Minnesota, I felt I had worked long enough. (I had spent the previous twenty years at another institution.) I was also tired of being an administrator. I felt it was time for new faculty and administrators to move the department forward. I wanted some time for myself. In retrospect, I should have done it differently. I should have worked part-time for a while and then retired. That would have given me time to develop other interests. It was also scary not having a regular paycheck.

I am very compartmentalized in my brain. When I was home with young children, I focused on being a mother. When I went to work, even with children at home, I focused on work. I was a good role model. I did not feel my identity was tied to being a doctor or an administrator. My department was innovative, moving toward a medical model of psychiatry rather than the more traditional psychoanalytic model. The focus was on the team.

I like being good at what I do. I thought I would play golf or take up some other sport, but I did not want to work hard to do what I thought trivial. I always had other interests, like playing bridge, and these were enough.

I like what I am doing now; it makes me joyful. My boss is younger than my daughter, and I really appreciate her being in charge. I like seeing some patients, doing research and teaching.

Work was never my social life. There were only two women in my medical school class, and I had relatively few female colleagues after medical school. I had women friends outside of work, and because my husband was a non-physician we developed relationships apart from my profession.

Leaving my last position was not much of a struggle. I wanted my department to be in good hands and I think it is. I still feel connected. Sometimes it bothers me to see faculty appointments that I would not have made, but generally I feel okay about what is happening.

—*Paula Clayton, M.D., Chair, Psychiatric Department,. University of Minnesota Medical School*

Our self-talk provides a constant commentary on how we are doing. Internal dialogue can undermine us or lift us up. When we're floundering, old familiar refrains start playing in our heads about how we aren't good enough, smart enough, or rich enough, and some of the voices tell us that we are getting old and becoming useless.

Some women cope beautifully. Their lives move from work to retirement as easily as moving from one day to the next.

At seventy years old, I decided to retire from a fulltime professorship, teaching teachers on the undergraduate and graduate levels. How you feel about being retired has to do with how you define the term. Retirement is not having to keep up with things like meetings. I probably would not have retired if all I had to do were teach. I like that I don't have to deal with people or routines that constrain my activity. Wasting time is an important consideration. Time has become too precious to use for meaningless things.

Getting rid of the work structure was freeing. I never felt depressed. I like to pursue what I believe to be important in my own time frame. I am very active and involved, doing much the same thing I did before formally retiring. I pick and choose when and where I do my professional work.

I look forward to every day. The only thing I miss is the financial security that comes with steady employment. I am clear about what I consider good use of time. I am also clear as to who I am without titles, job responsibilities, or structure. People are not going to change me—I know when I am right and have no need to find affirmation outside myself.

—*Manon Charbonneau, Ph.D., former Professor of Education, College of Santa Fe*

For women who find a sense of self in situations outside of work, separation from work is less jarring and easier to manage. There is no cessation of self-reflection when they transition to retirement. The mirror before them stays filled with images of service to the community.

I, for one, never had a career in the sense that young professionals do today. After majoring in French at college, I took a bilingual secretarial course to acquire some marketable skills. I married and became a secretary—first to four professors at Harvard University and then at a French bank on Wall Street.

I first retired to embark on a career in motherhood! Looking back over the years I spent as an at-home mom raising three sons, I remain firmly convinced that motherhood is the best and most important career of all. It is surely the most challenging!

When our eldest son was a high school junior, my husband started his own business. With college tuition only two years away, I felt I needed to help with the cash flow situation. However, I had no desire whatsoever to return to office work and nine-to-five hours. I already had a fulltime job at home. So I made some inquiries, found some "clients," donned my blue jeans and started cleaning houses.

A housekeeper's pay was not good in those days, so I needed to add something else. My son told me about an opening for dining-room hostess at the nearby retirement community where he worked part-time. He thought that I would be great in the position. I dressed in a suit and went for an interview, old resume in hand. The man who became my boss told me I was overqualified for the job. I responded that I was not looking for a high-powered position, just something part-time.

I was hired and worked there for sixteen years. It was perfect for me. I loved being there, so it never seemed like a job. I knew all the residents and their families and thoroughly enjoyed the young waiters and waitresses who worked under my wing. To this day, whenever I return to that wonderful place, I am greeted with hugs and excitement and told how much I am missed. Actually, a part of my heart is still with all those people, even though I now live 2,000 miles away.

A third job fell into my lap: Welcome Wagon representative. This organization no longer exists, but was very respected in its day. Representatives called on new residents, as well as mothers-to-be and young women planning weddings, and told them about various services in the area—doctors, lawyers, hairdressers, bakeries, restaurants, banks, you name it. Women who had just moved to the community were thrilled to learn so much about local businesses. By the end of most visits, newcomers no longer felt lost, and I received a thankful hug. This was another people job and right up my alley. I did it for ten years.

I was busier at times than I'd have been in a job with regular hours. But I appreciated the flexibility of being able to set my own hours. The years passed. I did not become rich in these jobs, but the satisfaction more than compensated. Then my husband and I decided to move to Montana and start a new life. That's when I really retired!

> I wondered how I would adapt to a life of leisure. Well, I have had no problem. I love being free to do whatever I please, exercise on a regular basis and travel whenever and wherever I choose. I am happy, fulfilled, involved in volunteer church work and available for our children and grandchildren. It's a great life.
>
> —*Virginia Heyler, former Secretary, Harvard University*

There is no single blueprint for lifestyle change that works for everyone. Planning ahead is a boon for some, but others forego the planning and still seem to do beautifully. A few women can't conceive of the difficulty their sisters are having.

>  Life after retirement is extremely busy and rewarding. When I retired after twenty-eight years, it was for important family reasons. I was never depressed, although I did miss the faculty and the challenges I found in my work. But then I discovered many more challenges.
>
> I believe we use the word "depressed" far too often, unless of course we're referring to clinical depression. What causes me "everyday" depression is the racial hatred and conflict all over the world, the repression of women, hunger, and the abuse of planetary resources. And let me add, the doublespeak of politicians.
>
> I am a cynic and a skeptic and proud of it. At seventy-four, I've earned that right. Fortunately, I and my husband of fifty-four years have ongoing discussions and can dig into our past experiences. We have been there! So my cynicism is one side of a coin and the other is my sense of humor.
>
> I have met with my friends from work on important occasions and still feel close to them. I was one of those women who loved my work, put all my creativity into it, and received many personal rewards. While I worked, I attended the university at night and graduated at age sixty with Phi Beta Kappa and Summa Cum Laude honors. I had been expanding my horizons for a long time.
>
> Depression after retirement? Bah humbug!
>
> —*Sylvia Cooke, B.A., former Executive Secretary, Albuquerque Public Schools*

How we adapt to change depends in part on how well we know ourselves and the care we take to understand ourselves.

Celebrating my sixtieth birthday, fortieth wedding anniversary and retirement within weeks of each other was cause for reflection! September 11 was cause for reevaluation. The more I ponder the past, present, and future, the more convinced I am that my philosophy of life, my core values and my innate personality determine my reactions to personal, professional, social, and world events. My response to retirement, therefore, was rather predictable.

Science, rationalism, and humanism have dominated my life. Biology was my first academic interest and I became a high school biology teacher. The influence of biological concepts, however, went far beyond the classroom for me. My college senior theme focused on change and continuity, unity and diversity, and homeostasis, all of which informed much of my professional and personal behavior and still do today. I see myself as a member of the human gene pool and my life as part of evolutionary history. But I do not see the human race as limited by biological determinism. I have faith in the power of knowledge and the human potential. I am, therefore, positive in my outlook on life, and embrace the challenges of each new stage of my development. Retirement is a new adventure.

The sequence of marriage-family-motherhood-career-empty nest-career-retirement-family has worked for me. I have enjoyed every stage of my personal and professional development, which included five geographical moves (husband's transfers) and consequent adjustments. Each one brought excitement, change and professional advancement. Retirement is simply another stage that will bring new challenges.

The novelty of retirement has not yet worn off. I have enjoyed tremendously the luxury of leisure time, freedom from schedules, and lots of togetherness with my husband, who retired about six months before I did. We are both involved in a major renovation of our new home and welcome this new phase in our lives, which brings us full circle back to children and now, grandchildren. We are also more involved with our elderly parents, which provides a powerful impetus to contemplate our future and live each day as fully and joyously as possible.

How I live my life in the future will, in some ways, be more in tune with my real personality. I am more of an introvert and a quieter person than the job of school principal demanded. It required multiple social interactions (both positive and negative), crisis management and constantly being on stage. Thoughtful, research-based decision making and quiet, solitary reflection were luxuries.

Early in my administrative coursework, I took a personality assessment that indicated a high need for achievement and power and low need for approval. This was helpful information to me, professionally and personally, because I needed to balance my task-orientation with people-orientation. As principal of an elementary school, I had lots of help from those around me, adults who were naturally people-oriented, and children. I think I am a more balanced person today than I was in my early years as an administrator.

My self-evaluation at this point indicates a low need for achievement, although daily accomplishment and productivity are still desirable. My need for power has also diminished, and is now focused almost exclusively on my husband, with good humor of course. I continue to have a low need for approval, enabling me to do whatever I feel like doing! A need for affiliation and relationships with family and dear friends is strong, probably stronger than when I was a young adult.

Admittedly, I am in a transitional stage. Right now, my decision making is certainly not important to anyone but me and my husband. Choosing wallpaper is not like hiring teachers. Deciding on which oven to order is not like placing children with teachers. But I am actually enjoying the process, as superficial as it may be, and I do not even feel guilty. Once we have settled into our new home, my needs will change and my responses to retirement will evolve. I am not sure what I will eventually do, but whatever it is will be challenging, fun, and will keep me learning something new. I also know that I will not give up the freedom, leisure, and family togetherness I so relish now.

—*Phyllis Constan, M.A., Elementary School Principal*

Women really tend to think of the retirement phase as a new life. That's how Phyllis refers to it in this update.

 My new life began on July 2, 2002, when we moved into our new home here on the east coast. I wake up every morning with a view of the sun coming up over Peconic Bay. The first year was busy, with a wedding for our daughter, lots of household projects and travel. This past summer was crazy with constant visitors (overnight guests 71 out or 90 days). Our fifth grandchild was born on September 2, so this fall has been lots of fun. Our sixth is due in January. I'm loving my job as "Granny Phyllis." I'm also doing a little consulting for a search firm that places superintendents and other administrators.

*—Phyllis Constan*

So what is all the fuss about? The women in this chapter either moved into retirement with grace and agility or found new adventures upon retiring. Many were bolstered by positive attitudes. They moved out of their offices, unpacked their boxes, left the empty desk to someone else and welcomed this new stage of their life's journey. We can't stay in the sea of despondency forever and let precious time slip away. We take the first steps toward redefining ourselves when we stand before the mirror and refuse to be daunted by what we see.

### High Priestess

*It is evening.*
*Light and dark are swinging in the balance*
*And as the scales tip toward dark*
*Millions of stars spill into sky.*
*Centuries ago men addressed the firmament.*
*With line and angle, myth and animistic art*
*They affixed upon the stars their ancient auguries.*
*Tonight my mind will not fit into those designs made*
*Before the pyramids,*
*Before Plato,*
*Before me.*
*I have the right to read the starts,*
*To reject connect-the-dots patterns*
*That seem a limit to my soul.*
*In the West I see my mother's rocking chair*
*And to the North my father's saddle.*
*I connect the lines between the stars,*
*And find familiar points are the angled design*
*Of Navajo rugs we laid upon as kids*
*To watch firelight flicker from the coal stove*
*On the ceiling cave above our heads.*
*The Southern stars are a story my mother told*
*Of when the moon fell in love with the sun*
*And the stars grew small with jealousy.*
*I am an astrologer who has walked the stars,*
*Seen evening become the warm golden spill of morning,*
*And made my own magical mythology.*
*It gives me joy, keen and sweet,*
*To see my mother's kerosene lamp rising in the East.*

—Bonnie S. Bostrom

# A Closer Look
## Self-Reflection, Preparation and Planning

Thinking ahead to what retirement will mean causes us to focus much more clearly on what we are presently doing with our lives. We look at the meaning in our career and the way work provides sustaining structure. We begin to see ourselves a bit apart from the job. We become more objective and look at issues that we have been avoiding or postponing until we "have time" to think.

We're good at putting things off. We reason that as soon as we get the college degree, or find true love, or buy the new house, or land the promotion, then we will sit down and take some time for ourselves. We will figure out who we are and what we are all about. Then we wake up at fifty or sixty and realize how little progress we've made. We stand before the mirror of memory trying to find a new image of ourselves, or to understand the old image in a new way.

Sometimes I look at my hands and think with surprise, "These are my mother's hands." This sense of familiarity happens fairly frequently, due to the fact that my hands are very like my mother's. But a deeper identification occurs, too. It is as though a genetic cue is triggered that causes me to resonate at a psychic level, to make a spiritual connection. I miss my mother. Yet, as I go through this stage of life, I retain a sense of her, as though I absorbed so much of her while she was living that she now resides within me as a personal archetype.

She was a strong model, because she was a strong woman. At thirty-six, with five young children and few resources, she left her life as a rancher's wife in the northeastern corner of New Mexico and struck out to find her fortune. She became a teacher, earned a doctorate in English and was a professor emeritus when she retired. Retirement wasn't easy for her at first, not until she started writing. Then she flourished. She published two books, *Girl On A Pony* and *Lords of the Valley* before she died in 1998.

As I sit here at my computer working on this book, I am amazed at how strong a model she was. I, too, started my formal education later in life and I, too, became a teacher. And here I am in the beginning of my retirement writing a book. It's very strange to me that I did not notice the pattern right away.

Now that I reflect on it, this writing project probably evolved so naturally because I saw the process modeled for me. Mom was writing her books while I was working at the University of New Mexico. She lived nearby and was able to share her thoughts and let me read the latest chapter. She was a great inspiration to me.

Those who inspire us often become models. We want to be like the person who encourages us, who lifts our lives to a higher level, engendering in us a desire to achieve as they have. They show us it can be done. That was my mom in her seventies, with her yellow tablet and soft-lead pencil, showing me how to find meaning, purpose and joy in retirement by writing. Years ago I wrote this poem for her, never dreaming how deep the patterns really were.

### Migration

*We stand beneath the flame maples of fall*
*Arkansas is gold and fire lying at our feet in Mother's yard*
*Our shadows splatter; ink on leaf, as we plan for birds*
*The feeder will be high for viewing from her window*
*I lift the blocks and place their gray faces one on one.*
*We stop, caught by the patterned flight*
*Of great migratory birds,*
*Soundless, bound for home.*
*I bend to lift again and turn;*
*She should not see my tears drop upon the block.*
*In her house I check for latent danger,*
*Worrying over the sinister shift of throw rugs,*
*Slippery tile, and rumpled carpet.*
*Walking the short way to her mailbox*
*She teases, chides me to write.*
*I walk in other times when the child I was*
*Witnessed the beauty of her dreams.*
*Some dreams are finished, printed up,*
*And locked in time upon her shelves.*
*New dreams she reads aloud to me, poetry,*
*A book she is planning;*
*She is my muse.*
*I leave and this time I let my tears fall free;*
*It seems they comfort her.*
*Flying home,*
*I sense the force and form of the steps we take*
*Toward final migration.*

If my mother was a model in her living, she was certainly so in her dying. Diagnosed with cancer of the lung, she knew she had little time and so she spent much of it organizing for her departure, planning final wishes and orchestrating her funeral. She managed to incorporate her dearest friends as part of the ceremony. Each of her children would say their goodbyes, her favorite musician would play Amazing Grace on the banjo, the minister she had known for years would come from Arizona to Kenton, Oklahoma, to preside, and a longtime friend would come from Arkansas to do her eulogy. We all got so wrapped up in planning the event that it took the edge off knowing that she was truly leaving.

She went into crisis late one afternoon in May. When we discovered that she had not signed her living will, my sister brought it to her and urged her to sign, so resuscitation attempts could be discontinued. Even after she had signed the document, they kept her oxygen on and so, with singular determination, she reached up and took off the oxygen mask and left, under her own power at her own time.

And so I write. I write to find meaning during this transition and to collect the stories of other women who are mid-stride between work and new ways of being in the world.

Millions of us are leaving the workforce at the same time. I believe that the same strength and competence that served us when we entered and became successful in the workforce can help us to address larger, more global concerns. We will do this by becoming models for younger women. I do not believe it is vainglorious to want to change the world, to apply our energies to social problems through activism and community-building. We are an unusual group of women. We can accomplish unusual things in the world.

—Bonnie S. Bostrom

Some women decide to make work and life a synthesis. Some professions lend themselves better to this than others. It would be difficult for a ballerina to keep on toe forever, but she could choreograph. A surgeon can't perform just a "little bit" of surgery on the side, or a pilot fly forever, but perhaps they can teach. However, some women have the best of both worlds.

Leaving the workplace doesn't appear to bring drastic change to women who are able to stay involved in their profession and to continue nurturing relationships developed at the workplace. The transition finds them in much the same place they were before they retired. They may not be getting a paycheck, but they have a retirement fund and are still doing the same work they were doing before they retired. Furthermore, they maintain vital connections with the people they knew, and these linkages help them maintain a consistent sense of self. In a way they just extend and expand into their own lives, using the freedom of retirement to develop more fully the relationships they had already begun. Some women move into retirement not as a falling star, but as a comet blazing a new trail.

After I retired and no longer had a business card to share with people, there were moments when I thought, "Who am I now?" For thirty years I had a title. Now I did not.

However, this was temporary. I accepted a volunteer position as Executive Director for New Mexico Association for Curriculum Development (ASCD), and voila, a business card again. I wanted to stave off a "blank" on my resume under work experience should I decide to work again. I served on the executive council for International ASCD as well. I hung in there for five years after I retired, though with every meeting I grew more inclined to stop.

Retirement has been wonderful to me. My husband and I continue to travel and I regularly get together with friends from the schools where I was assistant principal and principal.

This has been important to me. It keeps me in touch with who I was. I carefully choose what I want to do next, whether to be on a board or serve on a committee. I do not commit unless it agrees with my current life mission. This helps me prioritize my activities. Maintaining my physical, mental, spiritual and social being keeps my life rich with diverse experiences.

We are not defined by what we do for a living as I thought we were when I first retired. We are defined by who we are, what we can contribute, what we become, and by how much we enjoy. We can still make a positive difference with what God has given us.

—Bettye Bobroff, Ph.D., former Assistant Superintendent, Bernalillo Public Schools, Bernalillo, New Mexico

We recreate ourselves if possible, or create new ways to be ourselves. We adapt and make do. Sometimes challenges force us to live in an entirely new way. We drop deep within ourselves and find resources we didn't know were there waiting to come back to life.

 I now have a forceful happiness, not the soft happiness of a child that can be taken away at any moment, but permanent joy and balance. Many of my friends have divorced very good partners because they skidded off the rails when they left work. Maybe that's why I got divorced myself.

I'm on my own now and on the road. This lifestyle gives me the opportunity to think about myself, about my experiences and what they mean. I would recommend it to anyone.

I speak to women's groups, and many audience members are convinced they could not do what I do. They see that I am in remission from scleroderma, and just lost a finger to gangrene, but I assure them that it doesn't change a thing. The only difference is that when I book an airline flight, I also book a wheelchair so that I don't get tired walking through the airport. It's a free service and no one seems to mind.

When I tell the women my itinerary—North Africa, Australia, Europe—they think that it takes a lot of money, but it doesn't. I mostly stay with friends and they always seem to need something. I arrive just in time to house-sit or take care of a child.

My life is my work now. I write a lot. I'm in my sixties and feel retired. I notice three distinct aspects of myself: a childlike quality, my friendly ego and my absolute self, or connection to God. They seem equally strong. All parts of me feel more smooth and harmonious. This has happened since I've been traveling. Having little money has helped me to be realistic and embrace all aspects of myself.

I was the manager of a music studio. When I divorced my husband, I lost my job, then my home and all my possessions. Within a year I was reduced to what I could carry. I was depressed and had frightening angina. I felt that I might die at any moment. I even thought about suicide, but the love I felt for my children kept me from that. My husband told me that I was no longer in his heart and that crushed me.

It seems that all my life I've been starting again. I have found that I can live on very little. Friends have given me little gifts of money. In exchange I give something of myself. I've traveled to Australia, North Africa and Europe and even after absences of several years, I visit dear friends, and we pick up where we left off. I guess you could say I'm a bag lady.

—*Felicite Woods*

We retire from many roles in our lives. At one time or another we may be a boss, mother, wife, or volunteer. Some of these roles are permanent. We will always be somebody's daughter or mother. Other roles are impermanent and they remind us of the even greater impermanence of life. It is this ephemeral quality of our existence that sometimes lies at the bottom of the sadness or depression we feel when the roles we so cherished are given up or taken away.

Because we are retired does not mean that we are through. My writing partner, Barbara Reider, has been able to develop new ways of getting her needs met and new ways of viewing who she is.

 It has been over two years since I left my position as chair of the education department at the College of Santa Fe. I have hated the word "retire" since day one of this journey. When people asked me about retirement I would reply, "I did not retire, I just left my job." It was really important not be identified with the "retired." To me the word equated with old age, golf, endless and meaningless time. I refused to consider vacations whose brochures showed gray haired, even young-looking gray haired, participants. I immediately went into partnership with a colleague from the college. She is about ten years younger than I. We started a consulting business in the year following my retirement. The work was interesting. Then we created a nonprofit focused on professional development for teachers. I taught as adjunct faculty in my former department and, later, at other institutions of higher education in the area. Actually, I was pretty much back to where I'd been before I became a fulltime faculty member. I was working about the same number of hours and teaching in the same number of places, with a separate prep-bag for each course and each institution. The joke was making sure I had the right bag as I left each day, so I would not face a Wednesday class with a Saturday bag.

As busy as I was, I could not understand why I felt depressed. I was still active, doing many things I liked, so what was the problem? I discovered that I was reconstructing my life as it had been before I even considered retirement. The depression came from being out of balance and focused entirely on work. It has taken quite a lot of time and reflection, but I am beginning to piece together what I want my life to look like at this time. My teaching has become much more focused and, from what my students say, infused with passion. I am also teaching and mentoring a former student. I take considerable joy in watching her grow and develop. At first I felt envious of her. I wanted the social and intellectual connections of the workplace, the ability to create new programs, the feeling of control. However, the more I watch the more I realize that it is really her time now. My role has changed. I am free to teach what and where I wish. I like that I

can work my schedule around my vacations, rather than the other way around. I still feel holes in my life, but I don't push. Whatever comes next will get here. I am no longer young and, were it not for my friendly colorist, would most certainly be gray. I guess I will adjust and realize that age has benefits.
                                                    —*Barbara Reider*

Yes, every age has its benefits. We need to work at throwing away the value systems thrust upon us by our culture. We may never be thin again or have hair the color it was when we were in high school. Life is difficult and aging is hard. And yet, these stories speak of the heroics of women who in the midst of transition have the bravery to examine the dimensions of these changes and share them with each other.

Remember Bettye Bobroff's encouraging words: "Retirement has been wonderful for me." Wonderful in part because Bettye discovered a timeless truth: "We are not defined by what we do for a living."

A meta-narrative, a deeply embedded archetypal story lies behind all tales in which the plot leads to a defining moment. Marriage, family, career, retirement—these roles and the stories hidden within them tell us that when some goal is achieved, all will be well. Women of this generation had *True Romance* magazine and the Ginger Rogers and Fred Astaire movies to teach them about happy endings—the kiss, the ring, the baby. Then the Katherine Hepburn and Bette Davis movies demonstrated that we could be happy outside the constraints of the too-binding wife and mother narrative. The lives of the stars led us away from tradition into affairs, divorce and scandal. We followed in hot pursuit of adventure and freedom. The postwar days saw us working in new jobs, new industries and new cities, but the meta-narrative didn't really change.

The same invisible frames predicated our perception of who we were and what would make us happy. We expected to achieve the same goals of love, marriage and family while holding down a job as well.

Having crossed gender lines at work, we accepted the new corporate ladder to success, never realizing that it was a readymade hand-me-down from men. Maybe that's when women started to become angry, when the incidence of depression in women started its upward J-curve. We didn't have a chance to create a world of work for ourselves, but merged into the work world of men and now, when we leave that world, we go back into the more traditional world of women. We are expected to volunteer, do service work and be active grandmothers, but for women who were never comfortable with traditional limitations, these roles just do not work.

Some of us did not marry. The prince wasn't the answer because we wanted the princess ourselves. We crossed more lines, struck down more confining structures. We were childless or had children by artificial insemination. We formed two-mom families, single-mom families and traditional and non-traditional families. Many of us chose to be alone. We like the solitude and freedom of the single life, though it may seem alien to our sisters surrounded by children and grandchildren. Being a granny isn't the be-all, end-all for some of us.

We are rarely fully ourselves, so the opportunity to be with the one person we neglected for our entire lifetime, our self, may not sit well, may even be boring. Remember, we had all that serotonin going for us at work, not to mention the power, prestige and long lunches with dear friends.

It's ironic that we commonly give retiring colleagues a watch. Perhaps we are saying: now your time belongs to you and not to the company. That weight of time is what women seem to be addressing with plans to take courses, travel and garden. If we took a yearly planner and filled in every hour we intended to spend gardening, taking classes and travelling, there would still be hundreds of hours to fill.

Filling time with activity is not necessarily the answer. We must choose very specific, meaningful kinds of activity that utilize our brains and support feelings of status.

Other kinds of pain attend the calamitous change we call retirement. The pain that stops you for a moment at the door to the dentist's office, before you even enter, or hits when you contemplate the blank space behind "occupation" on the health form. You run through the mental files looking for your label, your title, something that legitimizes you as a person. It can hit when people ask politely what you do, and you stand there with the feeling that since you are not a "something" you must be a "nothing." In a vague attempt to explain, you offer, "I was…" or "I used to…" If you respond by saying "I'm retired," most people want to know what you used to do, not who you are now. Or they politely say, "Oh, that's nice," and run away to freshen their drink. With a bit of luck you will run into another recently retired person and the two of you will talk intimately about your shared metamorphosis from professional to person.

Our dreams may be too tied to our work life. Perhaps we should try dreaming new dreams, embracing thought from other cultures and widening our personal vistas. Western culture has a hard time accommodating other cultures unless they, too, are built around work. In particular, it is hard to understand the culture of countries like Tibet, where individual work and aspiration seek to enlighten not only the self, but others. A person's highest ambition is to transform the self and to relinquish any sense of fixed identity. In our culture we work to secure a fixed identity and use our professional stature to assure ourselves that we *are*, that we *matter*, that we *mean something*.

When we leave work, we leave behind the identity that evolved in that particular environment. For many of us, leaving may precipitate more than an identity crisis. It may create a spiritual crisis as well.

*10*

# Uncovering the Mirror
## Discovering the Spirit Within

What is left when we sense our old identity dissolving around us? What is the force that we sense deep inside the dark mirror, calling, beckoning us to look, to see? When the cloak of illusory identity drops away, only the internal self remains. That is what we face in the mirror: the self, stripped of the familiar adornment and safety of our professional identity.

We think of youth as a time to discover our truth, a time to seek spiritual sustenance. The image of a woman embarking on a vision quest at fifty, sixty or seventy does not readily leap to mind when we picture the search for spiritual truth.

The poets, philosophers and sages belonged to our youth, when we searched for the meaning of life, knew angst and thirsted for God. Somewhere along the path to enlightenment, we found ourselves immersed in the mundane business of living. We became consumers, parents and homeowners. Instead of reading poetry, we grabbed precious moments for ourselves and wrote a few verses, reconnecting for a moment to the time when we were filled with wonder and wanting.

As unlikely as it may sound, when we leave our work behind we enter a period very much like that youthful time when we were open, vulnerable, and not quite so fixed in a sense of identity. Age erases the painful memories of that time, the tumultuous emotional wavering of the spirit as we looked for religion, or escaped from the religion of our parents, or just yearned to be safe in some belief system.

Our spirits have been on hold, waiting to move out of the cocoon of work to continue the quest. Like new life emerging from the chrysalis, we unfold our wings and move toward full spiritual development as women.

 Leisure is an essential part of Benedictine spirituality. It is not laziness and it is not selfishness. It has something to do with the depth and breadth, length and quality of life. The six weeks prior to my retirement in 2000 was Lent. The book, *Wisdom Distilled From the Daily: Living the Rule of St. Benedict Today* (Chittister, J.D., 1990), was the Lenten study at First Presbyterian Church where I belong. The author includes a chapter on leisure, Holy Leisure.

I was deeply moved by the author's explanation of the importance of leisure and literally condemned by my neglect of it for so many years. Not that I was ignorant of the need for stress release through vacations, hobbies, exercise, proper diet, rest and meaningful spiritual practice. I had, in fact, tried hard to incorporate all of these practices and often at the same time. But Holy Leisure was different. Those words captured my thoughts. I began telling everyone that I was, "embarking on Holy Leisure," not merely retirement, and that I was so far behind, if I lived to be a hundred I could probably never make up for my negligence. But I would sure try.

For eighteen years I directed a preschool, childcare and kindergarten program. Challenging hardly describes this often thankless work. But I loved administration. I was good at it and I enjoyed meeting all kinds of people. I had a passion, a calling. I was driven to attain excellence.

The tasks of a nonprofit, early-childhood director are greatly diversified, stressful, certainly not boring. I never knew when I left home in the morning if I'd play the role of director all day, or fill in as plumber, janitor, grant writer, gofer, mediator, referee, detective, boss, bill collector, cook or teacher-aide. Being the director meant playing all those roles and then some. But that was okay. At least I wasn't stuck at a desk doing the same old thing day-in-and-day-out.

About two years prior to my decision to retire, I began to notice that the days when I felt a bone-deep weariness were coming closer and closer together. My blood pressure was out of control, my patience was zilch, I was short-spoken with staff, parents and even board members. I was irritable and exhausted. The thought would come to me several times a day, "I'm ready to go home," or "I am so tired of this."

Work was no longer fun or exciting. Mornings found me dreading the day. My profession had become drudgery, a job to be endured. Every minute of the workday seemed to demand my immediate attention. A large portion of my time was spent putting out fires and what had previously seemed like moderate problems were now in my mind major crises.

A lack of sufficient qualified staff limited my ability to find creative ways of directing, to test new ideas, or even maintain the status quo. I could hardly muster the energy just to get through the day. I was totally burned out.

Two weeks before my sixtieth birthday I attended a mandatory Saturday training session, feeling quite perturbed that I had to give up part of my weekend. At that session I learned that I did not have to remain director for two more years in order for the school to remain accredited, as I had thought. As long as the school had a qualified director, that hard-earned recognition would continue.

I could hardly wait to get home to write my letter of resignation giving six weeks notice! Just as I had known in my heart that I fit the position when it was offered to me years before, I knew when it was time to go. I was just as excited about leaving as I had been about beginning!

The eighteen months since I retired have been filled with bliss, delight, and wonder. I often marvel at how blessed I am, how lucky I am to be able to live the kind of life I love. On some mornings I turn over and sleep another hour, daydream over a second cup of coffee, or agonize over the news. Most mornings I'm out of bed fairly early, spend quiet time and then go for a long walk. I have leisurely lunches with old and new friends, read my collection of books and magazines and surf the Internet. Studying and learning have always appealed to me. Gardening is a hobby, and I've taken a master gardener course, which also requires ongoing community service.

I have time to travel, primarily to visit friends and family, although I prefer staying at home. I play the piano daily, a practice sidelined long ago by two daughters and all those unending duties required to keep some semblance of an orderly household. We usually eat at home, more healthfully than before.

Volunteering weekly at a public school has been quite rewarding as have days spent working on a Habitat for Humanity house. I serve on several church committees, teach Sunday-school preschoolers and participate in three study groups, one on feminist theology. Through all these activities I continually meet new people, young and old, and have time to get to know many of them on a personal level.

As I pondered retirement, I was never apprehensive about what I would do with the years of unstructured time, or about who I would become, although self-identity was an issue for me as a young wife and mother. At this stage of life my attitude is different, because I am different. I have proved myself to me.

> —*Malissa Haslam, former Director, Preschool/Childcare/Kindergarten,
> Santa Fe, New Mexico*

The spirit seeks nurturing. We don't always know in what form sustenance will appear, or what our responses will be. A bell sounds, a passage in a book speaks to us with new resonance, we remember something a parent said when we were young and our spirit moves, reminding us of its journey.

As we move into retirement we are also moving into the full-bloom season of our lives, when events will occur that are natural, but devastating. We may lose spouses, beloved friends, or our health. Eventually we will lose our lives. These realities are at the forefront of consciousness as experiences speak to the fragility of life, the tenuous hold we have on our destiny.

While calamitous, such events can be opportunities for expanding, learning compassion, being of service to others and deepening our appreciation for beauty, kindness and humor. We can learn to face our fears of death and dying.

 For me, retirement means circling the wagons and making myself safe from the coming onslaught.

I have worked for twenty-five years in the mental health and social service field and have accumulated almost no retirement benefits. Most of the time I have been self-employed and too involved in the moment to be mindful of the need to save. So here I am at sixty-one with no plans to retire and the intention to move deeper into life within my community.

Two years ago I bought a 1927 two-story colonial home with four bedrooms and a huge living room with fireplace. Slowly it is becoming a comfortable and welcoming space where I can see clients, entertain my children and grandchildren and teach workshops. I frequently have eight-year-olds in the kitchen rolling out sugar cookies, and invite masters and teachers in to share perspectives on spirituality, psychology and mythology. I love where I am right now.

I admire the poet Mary Oliver, who writes, "...To live in this world one must do three things, love what we love, hold it close to our bones as if our life depends on it, and when it is time to let it go, to let it go." I am moving deeper into my life, widening my circle of friends, letting go when I must and encouraging new people to come in, especially children.

I opened my home to over one hundred seniors during a parlor tour our arts council sponsored this Christmas. I loved watching their faces as they studied pictures of European ancestors hanging on the walls, my mother's antiques, polished and sitting throughout the house, and the fire blazing warm in the fireplace. In this house, one can go anywhere, investigate and touch everything. I am so happy to open my arms and say, "Explore everything."

This spring I will host a wedding for my niece. My family will hold their reunion here. Two Russian businessmen will stay here for ten days while they visit our community.

I teach one night a week in a masters program for therapists and maintain a full private practice. Nights when I am not teaching I watch NBA basketball, thriving on my Sacramento Kings, delighting in their team chemistry. When they shoot and do not make a basket, they don't whine and cry and hire a therapist. They run back down and reposition themselves to try again. This has become a metaphor for the way I currently guide my life. You do not make every basket and you do not miss every shot!

I belong to the Rotary Club. This spring we will be developing a program to raise money for underprivileged children. We shepherd a school populated by neglected children from poverty-stricken homes. We have donated a washer and dryer so they will have clean clothes. We buy clothing, supply meals and give bikes and toys at Christmas. This diverse school is near my home and very dear to my heart. Many of the children have special needs. To raise money, I am planning a huge dance—a junior prom—with a retro theme and a big dance band. Who does not want to relive their junior prom with the wisdom of years, and who does not need to have fun?

I am in my retirement years and my life is full. Ideas and energy are abundant! I want to hold this life as close to my bones as I can and let this body live fully. Then, when it is time to let it go, I will let go.

—*Katherine Moore, M.S.W., Counselor and Certified Hakomi Therapist, Marysville, California*

Letting go. How many times have we confronted the need to let go of comforting habits because our doctor says that smoking kills, or coffee causes indigestion? How absurd that after years of eating all the sweets we wanted, we can no longer indulge lest we diminish our quality of life or, worse, die before we are ready.

Letting go of habits of the mind is even more problematic. The mind is given to rationalizations of immeasurable proportion. Furthermore, the pursuit is sometimes mistaken for the destination. We get caught up in the endless chase, taking self-development workshops, poring through the self-help section of bookstores, meditating, medicating and recklessly throwing ourselves into activities in the hope that something somewhere will extricate us from who we no longer wish to be. We become "try this" junkies.

If letting go is difficult at this age, "letting be" could be the antidote. We can be gentle when making adjustments and relinquishing habits that have grown dangerous, and we can be encouraged that this time, this wonderful last season, is the season of the soul. As the caterpillar draws into itself, builds its cocoon, dissolves into living liquid to become a crystalline being and emerges a beautiful winged creature of color and flight, we too can fly.

 I've never been afraid of growing old. In fact, just the opposite is true. When I was nine, I remember sitting on top a huge boulder, my thoughts captured by a billion stars as I tried to understand life, spirit, and the longing I felt.

I remember the tears as I waited for the coming of the elder. I saw her often in my dreams, begged her to take me away and teach me about wisdom and spirit, to help me understand all my heart knew to be true about life, love and living.

She never came. So I found myself silently watching and learning from the elders our culture put to waste, waiting for the day I too would be old enough to be watched by a small child trying to understand her world. At forty-two, I welcome with excited anticipation the years of my crone.

Retirement has never been a household word. People in my family simply do not retire. They get old. I watched each of my grandmothers live their passions, stopping only when their bodies no longer allowed it. My father, at seventy, is still dedicated. It has never occurred to me to think about retirement, only about aging and life and what the two will bring when they join as one. In the meantime I constantly remind myself to find and live my passions.

Aging brings the excitement of knowing that, as each year passes, life becomes richer in meaning and adventure, as though the culmination of all the years adds breadth and depth to each new experience. Listening to tribal elders share their stories helped me to understand that each moment lived is a moment to cherish. I remember their dreams and hopes and the faraway look that would mask their faces when they talked of regrets. I witnessed tears of sadness as they remembered the fear of daring to love, the fear of daring to seize each moment to be fully alive. They taught me that we have only one chance to live our dreams, one chance to love with an open heart.

When I find myself fearful of dying, I remember the elders. I remember that more fearful than death is the fear of daring to love, the fear of daring to be alive. I am reminded of the writer, Oriah Mountain Dreamer. "…I want to know what you ache for, and if you dare to dream…I want to know if you will risk looking like a fool for love, for the adventure of being alive…"

Thank God I was born the fool. Life is far too short to forget that we humans have an opportunity for extraordinary life upon this planet. I have spent my first forty years preparing to live the last forty as fully and with as much love, compassion and laughter as I am capable. Knowing that half of my life is complete and that I could at any moment take my last breath, I ask myself, "What would I regret?"

I don't think about retirement. I think instead about who I want at my side when I die, what dreams I want to take with me, what experiences I want to have solid in my bones. I want to know that I have shared the laughter of my soul and the tears of my heart with others and that I have tasted the beauty of their souls and the sweetness of their presence. I want my children to know they are the loves of my life.

It occurred to me one day that when we die our souls will be filled with the experiences of our hearts. We will take the richness and the fullness with us, not the joy or the pain. When I sat in front of His Holiness, the Dalai Lama, his eyes smiling, staring into my own, I understood that the only thing that would stop me from loving was fearing how many times I could dare to dare before my heart would break. When I fear to dare, I am choosing to embrace regret.

I find myself building a circle of friends and family, a foundation to cradle my soul each time I experience the exquisite wonder of the human heart. A circle of friends who also dare to brave their passions and their souls, risking the fool for love. It is with these people that I welcome the coming years of my crone, knowing that through them I have the strength to dare my core to waken and shake loose my soul for love. Should my heart break, they are there to open the belly of the universe with the laughter of experience.

—Jenny Lemire, *Hakomi Teacher and Therapist*
*Seattle, Washington*

Shodo Harada Roshi compares the original mind of human beings, the mind we have at birth, with a clear mirror, pure and uncluttered, with nothing in it whatsoever—without shape, form or color. If something comes before it, the mirror reflects it, but the mirror itself gives birth to nothing. If the reflected object leaves, its image disappears, but the mirror itself loses nothing. Within the mirror there is no birth, no death. No matter how dirty the thing reflected, the mirror does not get dirty, nor does it become beautiful because something beautiful is reflected in it. The mirror doesn't get dirty, clean or beautiful. Just because something is reflected doesn't mean anything increases in it either, nor does anything ever decrease. A mirror is without increase or decrease.

Each of us will, when we are ready, reach up and uncover the darkened mirror. Light will strike the reflective element making it translucent and we will see a familiar face, perhaps changed in subtle ways by our life's incredible journey, but familiar. It is that unchanging self, looking back at us from deep within the mirror that we recognize. She is all that is important and she has been there all along, waiting for us to arrive.

# References

Bolen, Jean Shinoda, M.D., *Goddesses in Everywoman: A New Psychology of Women.* Harper Collins, New York, NY, 1984.

Chittister, Joan D., O.S.B. *Wisdom Distilled from the Daily: Living the Rule of St. Benedict Today,* pp. 95-107, Harper Collins, New York, NY, 1990.

Dreamer, Oriah Mountain, *The Invitation,* Harper San Francisco, 1999.

Hanners, LaVerne, *Girl on a Pony,* University of Oklahoma Press, 1994.

Hanners LaVerne, *Lords of the Valley,* University of Oklahoma Press, 1996.

Kent, Brad, Contributor, *2001 Mission Yearbook for Prayer and Study: Let Justice Roll Down Like Waters,* p. 337, Presbyterian Distribution Service, Louisville, KY.

Konigsberg, E.L., *From the Mixed Up Files of Mrs. Basil F. Frankweiler,* New York, Atheneum, 1967.

LaCerra, Dr. Peggy and Bingham, Roger, *The Origin of Minds: Evolution, Uniqueness, and the New Science of the Self.* New York: Harmony Books 2002.

Oliver, Mary, New and Selected Poems, in *Blackwater Woods,* p. 177, Beacon Press, 1992.

Shodo Harada Roshi, "Original Mind" http://onedropzendo.org/origmind.htm.

# Self-Help Exercises

If you are a woman facing retirement, you have probably done the necessary financial planning without giving a great deal of thought to emotional and psychological preparation. Major life changes are frequently accompanied by feelings of loss and grief. A lengthy and painful transition period is sometimes required between the old life and the new. While conducting the interviews for this book, it became apparent that most women do not have access to tools for handling the emotional trauma that sometimes accompanies retirement.

The exercises on the following pages are offered to help you prepare for your life after retirement. Several of the women we interviewed came up with unique ways of coping with change. I have included their activities and added others. It is my hope that these exercises will help guide your thinking and give you a starting place on the new adventure before you.

Two types of exercises are included, those that call for individual work and those that require working with another person or a group. You may want to use the group-work exercises as a curriculum for retreats or workshops.

Deal with the most critical issues first. This will help eradicate any fears brought on by negative fantasizing. Remember this acronym: FEAR = Fantasized Events Appearing Real. Not knowing what action to take, or where to start, leads to unproductive and often unnecessary worry.

## Individual Exercise #1
# Journal Questions

Set aside time to reflect on the following questions. Read all of the questions before you begin to answer them. This will give you an overview so that you can start wherever you think best. When you are ready, write your answers in a journal. If you do not enjoy keeping a journal, merely contemplate the questions and use them as organizing tools. Refer to your answers from time to time to see if your assessments have changed and to judge progress toward your goals.

### Age
1. What is a realistic time frame for accomplishing future goals?

2. What type of support do you need to cope with issues related to aging?

3. What is the longevity of your parents, siblings?

4. What existing life goals may be compromised by your age?

5. What are some new goals you wish to set?

### Income
1. Have you met with professionals about your will, living will, trusts and general financial picture?

2. When do you plan to contact Social Security Administration to determine how much you can expect to receive?

3. Have you checked on the status of your 401K, Sep or Ira?

4. What plans do you have for augmenting fixed income?

5. What are your plans regarding future living requirements, e.g., assisted living or retirement home?

6. What health care policy will you put in place?

## Education
1. What do you truly want to do in the world that you haven't already done?

2. How can your retirement be organized to accomplish this dream?

3. Will further education be necessary?

4. Do you plan to pursue interests for which additional coursework is needed?

5. Are you considering an entirely new profession? If so, what?

6. What courses might you take just for the sheer pleasure of learning?

## Health
1. While you are still working, get baselines on all aspects of your health: hearing, vision, general health and special conditions. Use this as a starting point in tracking health changes over time.

2. Do you have a support system to help you manage the retirement transition? Consider investing in a few sessions of individual or group counseling. What about starting a support group with women colleagues who are exiting your workplace on or near the same date as you? Your human resources department may be able to provide assistance in locating such women.

3. Complete and sign a living will for your doctor and hospital.

4. If you have children, give them information about medications you are taking and any health issues that might require emergency attention.

## Family
1. What can you do to strengthen emotional bonds with family members?

2. Which if any family members would you like to live near?

3. What is your responsibility to extended family members?

4. What needs of your children must you take into account?

5. How much time do you plan to spend with grandchildren?

6. If your parents are living, how will you handle your relationship to them?

7. What are the expectations of your spouse or partner regarding your retirement?

8. In what ways will retirement make you more or less available to your partner?

9. What difficulties, if any, will your retirement pose for your spouse or partner?

10. What heretofore unspoken dreams, hopes or aspirations should you discuss with your spouse or partner?

## Environment

1. Are you living in your current home or locale because of your career?

2. In what other geographical areas have you thought about, or dreamed about, living?

3. If you plan to relocate, will you do so to help others, to fulfill a dream, or to receive needed support?

4. What changes would you like to make to your current home?
- Unpack boxes/get organized
- Organize professional papers/books/documents
- Remodel and/or redecorate
- Landscape or garden

5. What pets do you have, or hope to have?

6. What accommodations are needed for pets?

6. Who will care for your home, garden and/or pet when you travel?

## Spirituality

1. How much time do you plan to devote to spiritual reflection, introspection or expansion?

2. What activities will you use to deepen your spiritual practice?
   - Travel to cultural/religious places
   - Courses or seminars on religious/spiritual topics
   - Meditation, yoga, other disciplines

3. Are you interested in examining your particular religious heritage? How?

4. Would you like to study other religions or denominations? How?

# Individual Exercise #2
# Re-thinking Time

You may need to adjust to having considerable unstructured time, particularly if your work life has been highly structured. Whether you are looking forward to leaving work, or have already begun the transition, the following exercises may be helpful.

If you have used (or are still using) a day planner, take a look at how your days were generally organized. Calculate the amount of work time spent in the following categories of activity:

## On the Clock

1. Necessary phone calls

   _____hours/minutes.

2. Meetings

   _____hours/minutes.

3. Direct work application (teaching, litigating, surgery, etc.)

   _____hours/minutes.

4. Correspondence (email, letters, etc.)

   _____hours/minutes.

5. Preparation for direct work (research, lesson plans, etc.)

   _____hours/minutes.

6. Lunch/ Breaks.

   _____hours/minutes.

7. Travel (average daily)

   _____hours/minutes.

8. Other.

   _____hours/minutes.

## Off the Clock

Calculate time spent on work-related activities before and after work.

1. Planning

   _____hours/minutes.

2. Paperwork

   _____hours/minutes.

3. Correspondence

   _____hours/minutes.

4. Upkeep (dry cleaners, hair, nails, car, etc.)

   _____hours/minutes.

**Add up the hours.**

Now, think about how you will spend the same amount of time each day *after* retirement. You may want to shadow yourself for a few hours some weekend. Keep track of how long it takes to do routine things like cooking, eating meals, housework and errands. Be mindful of what you are doing and notice to what degree your thoughts are focused on some aspect of work. Give some thought to how differently you will be spending your time after retirement. Start planning what you will do with all the available time.

## Individual Exercise #3
# The Calendar Year – Life Mapping

Unless you're the kind of woman who is comfortable letting life flow spontaneously, life-mapping will help to orient you around particular goals. The intent of this exercise is to actually "see" the placement of blocks of time throughout the year, and to begin to come to terms with even larger blocks of available time.

If possible, generate several month-view calendars on the computer. These will provide ample space to map out your plans, month by month.

Let's say that during the first year of retirement you want to travel to Europe, create a spectacular spring garden, take an art course, participate in a weekly yoga class, and volunteer at a nearby school. The first step is to list these activities.

One at a time, take each item on your list and estimate the number of hours or days required throughout the year. For instance, to have a spectacular garden, you may need to prune and prepare beds during January and February, plant during March and April, and maintain the garden throughout the summer.

With a colored marker, make thin lines on your calendar to show the portion of each day you plan to spend on gardening and related tasks.

If you plan to travel, color in your projected travel time for the year. Do the same for volunteer work, courses, exercise, family events, etc.

Develop a color code, which will enable you to overlay projected blocks of time.

It will probably become apparent that, even after all of your activities are accounted for, much unstructured time remains.

If you are accustomed to an environment where every moment counts, be prepared for abrupt change. This exercise should help you prepare. Once you have your year mapped out, start planning how you will use all that extra time.

# Individual Exercise #4
# Achieving Balance

The purpose of this exercise is to assess the balance of opportunities for self-actualization provided by work and home. It will help you to define where new activities are needed to maintain equilibrium.

On a scale from 1 to 10 with 10 being high, rate the following with respect to your work life and home life.

| | At Work | At Home |
|---|---|---|
| 1. I can express my talents and specialized skills. | | |
| 2. I can utilize my education. | | |
| 3. I fulfill social needs. | | |
| 4. I interact with my closest friends. | | |
| 5. I am creative. | | |
| 6. I derive a sense of self-worth. | | |
| 7. I derive a sense of closure and gratification. | | |
| 8. I accrue status. | | |
| 9. I define my identity. | | |
| 10. I give to others. | | |
| **Totals** | | |

Take a good look at your ratings. Which areas need your attention?

# Individual Exercise #5
# Who Am I?

The purpose of this exercise is to help you clarify the differences between yourself as a *doer* and yourself as a *being*—the self as actor in the world and the self at rest. It may also help you understand how much you identify with specific roles. How others see you with respect to your roles influences how you perceive yourself. Take some time to reflect on the following questions. You may want to elaborate a bit in your journal.

1. What do I *do?*
2. What do people observe when I am *doing?*
3. Who *am* I?
4. How do others see who I *am?*

## Individual Exercise #6
# Dream Sorting

**1.** This exercise looks at your dreams. Examining those dreams you have realized, those you are ready to relinquish and those you are still pursuing may help you construct a new life plan. A dream is the precursor to a vision. Those of your dreams that have become concentrated visions have propelled you forward toward their realization. List here the dreams/visions you have realized.

**Dreams I have realized.**

---

**2.** Unrealized dreams can be difficult to relinquish. Fame, stardom, family, children, wealth—the list is different for each of us. Write down the untenable secret dreams that you are willing to let go of. It is important to do this work. Dreams not dealt with rob you of energy and clarity and keep you chained to the past. Be kind to yourself as you do this exercise. You may want to work with a friend. List the dreams you are releasing.

**I release these dreams, knowing they will not come to fruition.**

---

**3.** Next, revamp any forgotten or neglected dreams that need modification in order to be actualized. List here the dreams you are reconstructing to carry forward.

**I am reclaiming these dreams.**

---

**4.** In this section, appraise the dreams that you are still pursuing, e.g., a fledgling hobby, an educational goal, a spiritual or religious quest. List current dreams that you will continue to pursue.

**I will follow these dreams into the future.**

## Individual Exercise #7
# The Spiritual Quest

At last you may have time to truly explore your deep feminine nature. Some women travel to places where the sacred feminine has been honored. They visit temples in Greece to awaken the goddess within themselves. They explore India, Tibet, Egypt and the Amazon.

You don't necessarily have to travel to make a sacred quest or to explore facets of youself that may be richly rewarding. Use or modify the following ideas to suffuse your new life with the sacred.

**The Sacred Garden:** One woman is combining her love of statues and carvings of the Buddha with her love of gardening. She has been collecting for many years and now her trove of statuary is spilling into her garden. She took a master gardener class and is designing her environment to accommodate many of the larger pieces. Gardening has become more meaningful to her and her life is imbued with a sense of the sacred emanating from this combination of two loves.

If you do not have space for a garden, try container gardening (e.g., window boxes) or a simple herb garden. There is something extraordinary about going to your herb pots and harvesting fresh oregano, thyme, or lemon grass for your own cooking.

Embed special pieces of glass or stone in the soil around your plants. Nourishing your garden, no matter the size or type, will nourish you.

**The Sacred Space:** Create a special place in your home where you can go for quiet contemplation. It could be an altar, a meditation area, a corner of the studio where you paint, or even the top of a bookshelf. It can be a place for prayer, meditation or just sitting. The important thing is to create this place for yourself alone. Furnish it with treasures from your travels or daily experiences. A feather that falls on your walking path, a stone warmed by the sun—anything that speaks to you can become a part of your sacred space.

**Express Your Power:** The power you had in the workplace can be used in new ways. You may wish to align yourself with other people who are committed to causes that are important to you. There's a saying that in retirement men seek recreation and women go into politics. Regardless, use those great work skills to help your community.

Consider forming a consciousness-raising or support group for other women. Become involved in organizations. Many welcome new members. Your choice will depend upon your values, skills, and aspirations. So many of us are leaving the workplace at the same time, we can be a productive force in the world.

# Group Exercises

The following exercises and activities are particularly useful in a workshop setting. Most require little in the way of preparation or materials. By putting together a day-long retreat, you can provide women with a splendid opportunity to share their thoughts and experiences as they enter this phase of their lives.

## Group Exercise #1: Meditation
# Awakening the Heroes Within

**Purpose:** In this guided meditation on archetypes, participants identify untapped strengths and resources.*

**Materials:** None necessary; however, you might want to distribute copies of the meditation for women to take home and review.

**Preparation:** Have the women get comfortable and relax.

**Process:** Ask participants to find a comfortable place and take a few minutes to achieve a relaxed silence before you begin. Suggest that they close their eyes during this exercise.

Tell the group that you are going to lead a guided meditation on archetypes. Explain that archetypes are dynamic forces of the unconscious, patterns that have been present for so long in human history that some experts believe they are hard-wired into our brains. Suggest that interested participants research the writings of Carl Jung, who pioneered the work on archetypes, or the more recent work of Carol S. Pearson, from whom this meditation was adapted.

In a gentle but audible voice, slowly read the meditation, pausing for a few moments after each new direction:

*Sense deeply the resonance that occurs when an archetype lying dormant within you begins to respond. This signals an awakening of the gifts of that archetype.*

*If you are comfortable and ready, let us now begin to greet the archetypes within. Let there arise in you from the imaginary realm the archetype of the **Innocent**. This archetype gives us hope, helps to see silver linings and urges us to trust. Let this feeling of hope and trust move through your spirit and fill you with optimism.*

*Now release the Innocent and embrace the **Orphan**. She reminds us of our vulnerability and dependence on others. She helps us to develop compassion and empathy and allows us to voice our fears. We sometimes push her voice away from our conscious awareness. This is an* *opportunity to hear the message she has for you. Welcome her within, embrace her and let her become a part of you.*

The **Warrior** supports our sense of discipline, gives us courage in tough situations by helping us focus our intent and follow through to success. She is your strength, your resolve, your boldness. Accept her sword and her shield of protection.

As we greet the **Caregiver** we are reminded to give, to nurture and to sacrifice for others. She is our mother nature, our protector of loved ones. She lifts us up when our lives call for great action, and she is gentle in her manner. As we release her, let us remember to be a caregiver to ourselves.

The **Seeker**'s gifts to us are critical thinking, the will to leave untenable situations, and clarification of our identity. She pulls us ever closer to our true self. Our life is a seeking, and she is our light on the path.

We learn passion and commitment from the **Lover**. She recognizes beauty all around us and provides us with appreciation and love of life, people and work. As our external beauty changes form she shows us the path to our essence, where all that is beautiful resides. She is our source of energy and replenishment.

The **Destroyer** is valuable when it is time to let go of bad habits, projects and relationships. She helps us evaluate, organize and eliminate. She shows us how to approach challenges step by step.

Sister to the Destroyer, the **Creator** helps us take chaos and create structure and beauty. She helps us take ourselves in hand and shore up the skills we need to accomplish our dreams. She is there when we call upon her.

The **Ruler**, the great queen within us, assists us to take responsibility for our lives, to make tough decisions and to take action for the good of all. She causes us to volunteer, to champion the less capable, to work for harmony and reconciliation within the external community. Invite her to be with you as you begin any new venture.

The **Magician**, a high priestess, shows us possibilities and solutions. We have the power to transform situations and people as we expand our understanding. She helps us realize that problems are challenges— lessons to be learned. She is the strong advocate for win/win solutions. She understands the interdependent web of all existence.

We embrace the **Sage**, the wise woman we are becoming who helps us detach emotionally from old concepts and ways of doing things. She helps us hold sacred space for ourselves so we can hear our thoughts. She is before us, a beacon on the path.

*And last, the **Jester**. She shows us the fun in difficult situations, helps us laugh at ourselves. She opens us up to outrageous options and allows us to come up with ingenious and clever answers to dull, tedious problems. Keep her ever at the ready as your journey progresses, for she helps you find joy and grace in doing.*

*All these archetypes are part of you. You are a complex and amazing woman and you have all these tools, these aspects, these parts of yourself available to use, play with and enjoy. So take what you need— after all they are already in you. And now, when you are ready, please take a moment to reflect on which of these archetypes touched you most deeply. Which caused you to resonate most strongly? When you are ready to speak, say, "I now reclaim ____ and invite this part of me to be more active in my life." Fill in the blank with the name the archetype and briefly state why you have chosen to reclaim this aspect.*

After all the women have participated in this way, take another moment of silence to draw this activity to a close.

\* Adapted from *Awakening the Heroes Within* by Carol S. Pearson

## Group Exercise #2
# Photographs

**Purpose:** Participants identify qualities in a person they admire and have tried to emulate.

**Materials:** Ask each woman to bring a photograph of a special person who inspired her in some way.

**Preparation:** Provide plenty of space for women to work in pairs. If the weather is good, some may want to work outdoors.

**Process:** Have participants form pairs and find a quiet place to work. Instruct them to take turns showing the photo they brought and telling their partner about qualities in the person pictured that they admire and have sought to emulate.

After everyone has shared, bring participants back together to form a circle.

Next, have each woman report on what her partner found important in the person whose photograph she brought. Be sure to observe this important distinction: the women do not talk about their own photograph this time, but about their partner's. This enables participants to feel they have been heard and strengthens the rewards of sharing.

Bring the activity to a close with a few moments of silent reflection.

## Group Exercise #3
# Good, Bad, and Interesting

**Purpose:** This exercise encourages participants to think in more creative ways. It is based on the work of Edward de Bono, whose interest in lateral thinking has influenced education. Lateral thinking has been shown to facilitate creativity. Many of us tend to think in terms of black and white, good or bad. Edward de Bono believed that creativity lurks in the gray areas and can be teased out by treating questions differently, or laterally.*

**Materials:** newsprint, markers and easel

**Preparation:** Have participants form groups of four or five.

**Process:**  Spend a few minutes discussing facts and feelings associated with retirement. On the easel, begin to capture some of the statements made by participants. Examples are:

*I will miss all my friends at work.*

*I'll have lots of free time.*

*I'm afraid of getting bored.*

*I won't have to set my alarm clock anymore.*

As a group, go through the list of statements and decide if each statement is good, bad, or interesting. Put a G, B, or I next to the statement.

Ask participants to look again at each of the "B" statements, trying not to judge them. Ask: *Is there any way to change our thinking so that some part of the statement could prove interesting? How can we approach the statement creatively?*

Explain to participants that when they are able to suspend judgment about an issue or thought, they open themselves to creativity. Conversely, when they lock in the notion that something is bad, they construct a negative scenario. This is more than just looking for a silver lining. It is taking your present way of thinking about something and cracking it open to see if new and fresh ways of experiencing can be discovered. Not every statement on your list will be amenable to change, but if you can move some from the Bad category into the Interesting category, you will find yourself moving closer to happiness. Some statements that the group identified as Good may also be responsive to expansion and greater creativity.

* Adapted From *Cort Thinking* by Edward de Bono

# Group Exercise #4
# Escaping Dominant Ideas

**Purpose:** To help free participant thinking from limiting ideas.*

**Materials:** Newsprint, markers and easel.

**Preparation:** Have participants work in small groups. Announce that this exercise is adapted from the work of Edward de Bono.

**Process:** Explain that a valuable way to assess a situation is to explore the dominant idea in the situation and then escape from it. We have a tendency to fix on a dominant idea while ignoring related or divergent ideas. De Bono likens this to heading down a highway at full force, unaware that there are interesting side roads to explore. In order to find new ideas and derive new ways of being, we may have to escape from the main road, the dominant idea. For example, the dominant idea in running a railroad is to provide a transport service. However if we escape from the dominant idea, we can think of trains as offering entertainment—pubs, cinema, TV, or alternative housing. Likewise, the dominant idea of retirement is to quit working. By escaping from that dominant idea we can begin to think of retirement as a "start," not an ending—the start of a new career, the launching of a new project, the beginning of an exciting adventure.

Ask participants to discuss some of their dominant ideas about retirement in small groups. These ideas may be expressed as fears about retirement, or they may be focused on individual feelings of self-worth. Tell the groups to identify each person's dominant idea, honor that idea and then try to escape from it. Although positive, some ideas may be unrealistic. Participants should make an effort to escape from unrealistic ideas as well.

* Adapted from *Cort Thinking* by Edward de Bono

## About the Authors

Bonnie Bostrom, former Chief of Education for the Mashantucket Pequot Tribal Nation, holds postgraduate degrees in Special Education and Educational Administration and nurtured a passion for multicultural education and leadership development throughout her career. Upon retirement, Bonnie found herself in the throes of an unexpected depression. This book resulted from her courageous exploration of that experience and the experiences of other women facing retirement. She lives with her husband, Jim, in Florida, where she maintains a private practice as a Hakomi therapist, is an active communitarian, and delights in her two granddaughters.

Barbara Reider holds a doctorate in Human Development from Bryn Mawr College. She is the former Chair of the Education Department at the College of Santa Fe, from which she retired as Professosr Emeritus after ten years of service. She now teaches at Santa Fe area colleges and is a co-partner in Community Learning Collaborative, a nonprofit organization dedicated to educational reform.

# Surviving Breast Cancer

Foot Soldiers
Stories From The Breast Cancer 3-Day Walk
by Deborah Douglas, M.D.
With foreword by David W. Lounsbury, Ph.D.,
Memorial Sloan-Kettering Cancer Center

Retired pathologist, author, and breast cancer survivor, Deborah Douglas, M.D., walked 600 miles in 10 Breast Cancer 3-Day events to interview cancer survivors and co-survivors. The collected stories not only emphasize the complexity of diagnosis, treatment, and survivorship, but—due in large part to the emotional honesty of the contributors—challenge the popular mantras that a positive attitude is the only healthy way to cope with the disease and that cancer is an unequivocal gift.

## Read this book if you are:

- A cancer patient or loved one who wants to know how other patients handle the challenges of diagnosis, treatment, and survivorship and still find the courage to participate in a long-distance walk

- A health-care provider who wants cancer patients to understand that there are no right or wrong ways to face this disease

- Interested in signing up for a Breast Cancer 3-Day event, but want to know what it's really like to walk 60 miles, sleep in a tent, shower in a truck, and use porta-potties

- Simply curious why an otherwise perfectly reasonable middle-aged woman would leave behind her comfortable home, family, friends, and dogs to walk 600 miles in 10 cities

*The chapters deftly weave together incidents, observations, and conversations from the walks themselves; the stories of survivors and their families; the medical "journeys" of those survivors along with accessible technical explanations; and occasional incidents and insights from the author's own story. The writing is technically excellent, compassionate, humorous, and emotionally open. Everything about this book is exemplary.*

—Dianne Schilling, Instructional Designer

ISBN: 0944031 24 2

Aslan
PUBLISHING

www.AslanPublishing.com • www.the3-daybook.com
*Available nationally at bookstores and online webstores*

# MAXIMIZING ME

## What is your maximum potential? If you could reach the upper limits of your capacity to achieve and create, what would that be?

Early on, Hart Cunningham learned to focus his energy and talents on whatever creative endeavor he pursued. Through disciplined self-mastery he founded numerous still-flourishing global businesses, all by age 30. In this easy-to-read collection of lessons, he shares his hard-driving concepts and private axioms for personal success—the worldview of a determined individual, challenged to compete, to rise and to conquer all obstacles.

*Through Cunningham's insightful, dynamic learning process, you will:*

- Embrace your most outrageous dream and create the life map to reach it.
- Overcome any inertia that mires you in failed habits and choices.
- Reinvent yourself as the person you truly want to be.
- Resolve inner conflicts that divide your will and dilute your effectiveness.
- Reject egoistic self-deception and keep a clear fix on reality.
- Experience the vitality that flows from a clear sense of purpose.
- Follow a series of well-chosen goals all the way to your dream.

**Along with each chapter of advice, an exercise invites you to reflect, take action and transform your relationship with yourself and others.**

MBA Claremont Colleges CA at age 22. Hart launched his first global company at age 24. Challenging himself, more firms followed. They were featured in over 75 newspapers, including The Wall Street Journal and The New York Times. Twice, an Ernst & Young Entrepreneur of the Year® finalist, he is on the Chamber of Commerce CEO Roundtable Board, a think-tank and policy-making chamber of Fortune 500 officers, bank directors, and government officials. He lives in Arizona.

ISBN: 0 944031-99-4

Aslan
PUBLISHING

www.AslanPublishing.com • www.MaximizingMe.com
*Available nationally at bookstores and online webstores*